A LAYMAN'S GUIDE

To The

SABBATH QUESTION

DR. RICHARD P. BELCHER
REV. RICHARD P. BELCHER, JR.

Crowne Publications, Inc.
P.O. Box 688
Southbridge, Massachusetts 01550

Printed in the United States of America

ISBN 0-925703-43-5

CONTENTS

INTRODUCTION

Every reader probably has some conviction concerning the day of worship and how it is supposed to be observed. Such beliefs, no doubt, are the result of one's religious upbringing or teaching in the early stages of the Christian life, or from their own deep study of Scripture. For many the subject is settled. Others, on the other hand, are still wrestling with the issues. The present authors understand the difficulties of the task of seeking to determine one's position.

Important Issues

The place of the Sabbath commandment in the life of a believer demands one face many important issues.[1]

First, one needs to possess a growing knowledge of the teaching of Scripture since numerous passages in both the Old and New Testament must be examined.

Second, numerous areas related to the study of theology are necessary for consideration.

Third, different methods of interpreting Scripture will be encountered, especially as one begins to examine the relationship between the two testaments. A key question concerning methods of interpretation is, what relationship does the Old Testament law have in the life of the New Testament believer?

Fourth, the Sabbath/Sunday debate raises many ethical questions. Such key ethical questions include: What day of the week should be the day of worship for the church? How is that particular day to be observed? The practical implications of these questions have far-reaching consequences.

Fifth, the Sabbath question raises practical questions concerning how we are to apply the Sabbath commandment to our lives today. The importance of the question cannot be underestimated. Every believer who wants to honor God in every area of life will certainly be interested in whether or not the fourth commandment is relevant to worship and life today. If it is relevant for today, how should it be applied? Certainly every pastor and leader needs a clear understanding of the issues so that guidance can be given to congregations. Every pastor has struggled with the question of what to do with members who no longer attend worship services and spend their lives in other activities. Does the Sabbath commandment have anything to say to this difficulty?

These important issues surrounding the Sabbath/Sunday debate have arisen at various points in church history. On some questions there has been agreement, but on other questions there has been considerable disagreement. Even those within the same denomination or who adhere to the same theological viewpoint have not always seen eye to eye on this issue.

Basic Sabbath Views

The following chapters will center upon the question of the relationship of the Sabbath commandment to our worship practices today.

Certainly not all of the questions relating to this area of thought can be examined or explored. But some of the main arguments and passages of Scripture concerning three views will be set forth.

First the Seventh Day view will be discussed in Part One. It sees a direct relationship between the Sabbath commandment and our worship practices today. Two books by the same author, Samuele Bacchiocchi, serve as the basis for presenting this viewpoint. Those books are From Sabbath to Sunday and Divine Rest for Human Restlessness. Bacchiocchi was the first non-Catholic to graduate from the Pontifical Gregorian University in Rome. The first book mentioned above was his doctoral thesis. Bacchiocchi is a Seventh-Day Adventist who teaches Theology and Church History at the Seventh-Day Adventist affiliated Andrews University in Berrien Springs, Michigan.

Second, the Christian Sabbath view will be discussed in Part Two. It sees an indirect relationship between the Sabbath commandment and our worship practices today. This particular viewpoint is taken from various authors and articles. One book which takes this approach is The Christian Sunday written by Roger Beckwith and Wilfred Stott. Beckwith is warden of Latimer House, a theological research center in Oxford. Stott is rector of Croxton, Huntington, and has lectured in Bristol and Oxford.

Third, the Lord's Day view will be discussed in Part Three. It sees no relationship between the Sabbath commandment and our worship practices today. Two major works are used as the basis to set forth this view. Willy Rordorf wrote a book in 1962 which was translated into English in 1968. It was entitled Sunday and is regarded as a standard work concerning the origins of Sunday. Professor Rordorf taught Patristics and Early Church History at the University of Neuchatel in Switzerland. The other book, From Sabbath to the Lord's Day, was edited by D. A. Carson, Associate Professor of New Testament at Trinity Evangelical Divinity School in Deerfield, Illinois. This book began as a research project sponsored by the Tyndale Fellowship for Biblical Research in Cambridge, England in 1973. It was published in 1982. Although Rordorf and the authors of the Carson book do not always agree on some of the issues, they do agree on the fact that the Sabbath commandment has no relationship to our worship practices today.

Please understand that not every layman or scholar will find himself fitting neatly into one of the categories, and even though one may generally fit a certain category, he may not agree with all the convictions set forth by those of that viewpoint.

Many different principles and Scriptural passages will be examined in the following pages in order to set forth these views. The reader is encouraged to read this book with an open Bible so that God's Word is kept central in the midst of the discussions.

PART ONE

THE SEVENTH DAY VIEW

CHAPTER ONE

THE SEVENTH DAY VIEW

The Sabbath at Creation

The Seventh Day view, which will now be considered, holds that there is a direct connection between the Old Testament Sabbath command and our worship today. That is to say, the Sabbath command of the Old Testament is to be observed today in the New Testament period just as it was in the Old Testament times. This means the church today must worship on the Sabbath, the seventh day, and this day must also be a day of rest and service to God and others.

A leading advocate of this view is Samuele Bacchiocchi, a Seventh Day Adventist writer. The following chapters of part one of this work will be based on his convictions and arguments as found in his two primary books, <u>From Sabbath to Sunday</u> and <u>Divine Rest for Human Restlessness</u>. The first of these books is a very detailed presentation which considers the historical origins of Sunday as the church's day of worship. Bacchiocchi argues in this context that the Sunday observance of worship as practiced by so many believers today does not rest on a Biblical foundation nor on apostolic authority, but rather it grew out of later historical influences and factors.[1] In the second book he takes a more practical look at the meaning of the Sabbath in the Scriptures and its application for the church today. The following discussion will draw from these two books seeking to set forth his view and his defense against counter arguments to his Sabbath Day position.

Truths Revealed concerning the Sabbath and Creation

Any study of the Sabbath must begin with Genesis 1-2, the account not only of God's creation of the world in six days, but also the record that He rested on the seventh day.

Bacchiocchi sees this section of Scripture as extremely significant because it contains the first words found in the Biblical record about the seventh day. He considers the first words in the Bible on any subject to be a keystone to all later development on that given subject.[2] Several matters are clear for Bacchiocchi in his discussion of Genesis 1-2 and its teaching on the Sabbath.

First, the Sabbath celebrates human beginnings.[3] The Sabbath is introduced to us in these early chapters of Genesis between the two creation accounts, the first being found in Genesis 1:1-2:3 and the second in Genesis 2:4-25. Adam's first full day was the seventh day which he spent celebrating the inauguration of God's complete creation including the creation of man.

Second, the Sabbath signifies the presentation and assurance of abundant life. Usually when God blesses something He spells out what all that blessing includes. But in Genesis 2:3 the blessing of the Sabbath remains sealed as the text merely states, "And God blessed the seventh day, and sanctified it . . . " But in the unfolding of history, these seals are removed, Bacchiocchi contends.[4] God shows man that the blessing of the Sabbath in creation expresses His ultimate and total blessing over His perfect creation.[5]

Third, God declared the seventh day to be holy. According to Genesis 2:3, he sanctified it, indicating He caused it to be a means of holiness for mankind. Although the holiness of the Sabbath and the implications of that fact are not spelled out in Genesis, this holiness aspect becomes associated with the manifestation of God's glorious presence in Exodus.[6] What God initially promised His creation in the blessing and sanctifying of the Sabbath, which promise which centered on His glorious holy presence, He fulfilled in the sending of Jesus Christ into the world. Thus the Sabbath was created by God so that He himself might enter the world and sanctify it by His personal presence.[7]

Fourth, the Sabbath should definitely be seen as a creation ordinance. The command regarding Sabbath-keeping and Sabbath observance was never intended to be some temporary Jewish ceremonial law, but it is a permanent precept pertaining to all creation.[8] It is beyond question that the Bible gives vast significance to the creation Sabbath. It is set forth as a day of resting from work in Exodus 20. It is presented as a sign of the covenant according to Exodus 31:17. It holds a central place in the universality of the blessings of salvation.[9] Either Moses was guilty of a distortion of the truth or he was a victim of a gross misunderstanding when he traced the Sabbath back to creation and gave it such a prominent place in the life of God's people.[10]

Thus in light of the above factors, the Sabbath ordinance at creation is quite important. It celebrates human beginnings. It signifies the preservation and the assurance of abundant life. It was declared to be holy by God. It was a creation ordinance, which means it is to be a permanent observation.

Objections to the Sabbath as a Creation Ordinance

As Bacchiocchi sets forth his view of the Sabbath as a creation ordinance, he takes note of several objections and seeks to answer them.

First, someone might object to the Sabbath as a creation ordinance on the basis that the word "Sabbath" does not even appear in Genesis 1-2. How, therefore, could one speak of it as a creation ordinance when it isn't even mentioned in the Biblical text? For Bacchiocchi this is not a problem. The use of the phrase "seventh day" in Genesis may reflect the writer's concern to show the permanent existence and importance of the original sequence of days culminating in the Seventh day. Although the word Sabbath is not used in the creation account, it is introduced in Exodus in that historical and salvation setting.[11]

Second, someone might object to viewing the Sabbath as a creation ordinance on the ground that there is no command to observe the Sabbath in Genesis 2. Bacchiocchi would reply that though there is no clear enunciated command, there is the presence of a divine example in Genesis as God

Himself observed the Sabbath. And further, does this not tell us that it was God's intention for man to observe the Sabbath even before the fall? His intention was not that the Sabbath was to be an alienating command upon man, but that man would freely respond to his gracious Creator.[12]

Third, someone might object to recognizing the Sabbath as a creation ordinance in light of the fact there is no record that the patriarchs ever observed it. Bacchiocchi sees this argument as a giant fabrication of an anti-Sabbath argument. He points out that the tradition of the Jewish rabbis emphasizes the early origin of the Sabbath.[13] But that still leaves the question as to why it is not mentioned in Genesis. Bacchiocchi answers that the Sabbath was no doubt present but just taken for granted by the Biblical writer. He points out the existence of another period of time when there was a silence about Sabbath observance in the Biblical record, even though we know the Sabbath was observed at this time, that is, the period between Deuteronomy and 2 Kings. He suggests further that Genesis is probably concerned about sketching origins. Yet even Genesis, though it is silent on Sabbath observance, does mention seven day periods, which implies the existence of the seven day week, including the Sabbath. Also, in Exodus 16 and 20 the Sabbath is represented as an already existing institution.[14] Finally, Exodus 20:11 states clearly that the Lord blessed and sanctified the Sabbath at creation.

Conclusion

The conclusion of the matter, according to Bacchiocchi, is that unquestionably the Sabbath was established by God at creation as a creation ordinance. This means it is to be observed permanently by man. At the institution of this creation ordinance in Genesis God did not teach its permanence and continuance by divine command but by divine example. And though there is no evidence in the Biblical record that the patriarchs observed the Sabbath, Moses in Exodus 20:11 definitely traces the Sabbath observance back to creation in Exodus 20:11. Moses also in this verse records that it was sanctified by God.

Therefore, undeniably, according to Bacchiocchi, the actions of God and the events at creation and the rest of Scripture set forth the Sabbath to man as a permanent day of holiness to the Lord.

CHAPTER 2

THE SEVENTH DAY VIEW

The Sabbath in the Mosaic Law

No one can deny the place and importance of the Sabbath in the Mosaic Law. According to Bacchiocchi its importance and significance are clearly testified.

It was a part of the Ten Commandments, God's moral law.

It was a sign of the Mosaic Covenant.

It was a demonstration of Israel's love and fear of God.

It provided a starting point for all subsequent manifestations of divine grace.

It is a reflection of a healthy relationship with God for God's people.[1]

It speaks strongly of redemption or liberation. It denotes a covenant consecration (Exodus 31 and 20) and is a meaningful symbol of a covenant relationship.[2] In the Sabbath commandment of Deuteronomy 5 the people are told to remember the liberation they received from God.

It motivates the observer to be compassionate toward others. The result of understanding the liberation aspect of the Sabbath is that it will motivate the observer to show compassion toward others. Thus a proper understanding of Sabbath observance will not allow one to enjoy it at the expense of others but for the sake of others.[3]

It teaches one to center on the Lord on the Sabbath and not on himself. Proper Sabbath observance is not self-centered relaxation, but it is a divinely-centered rest to the Lord (Exodus 31:15) which frees a person from work so he can be free for God and others.[4]

It was a liberator of the oppressed. Both the Sabbath and the Jubilee years emphasized the release of debts, slaves and property. Thus it was a liberator of the oppressed.[5]

It possesses a political hope. Although the rest and peace of the Sabbath as a political hope remained largely unfulfilled in the Old Testament, it did become a symbol of the Messianic age often referred to as "the end of the days."[6] Isaiah uses the trumpet blast of the Jubilee year to describe the inauguration of the Messianic age (see Isaiah 27:13).[7] Thus the redemptive function of the Sabbath is seen as a picture of the mission of the Messiah (Isaiah 66:23).[8]

Conclusion

Thus according to Bacchiocchi the Sabbath in the Mosaic Covenant possessed a great importance. Not only was it a part of the Ten Commandments, but it was also a sign of the covenant. It demonstrated Israel's love and fear of God. It spoke strongly of redemption and liberation. Because of this liberation and through this liberation there came the result of selfless compassionate service to God and others. Finally it possessed a political hope as it looks to the Messianic age.

Thus in these first two chapters, Bacchiocchi has argued that the Sabbath is a creation ordinance which has also a strong place in the Mosaic Covenant. Consideration will now be given to Bacchiocchi's view of the Sabbath in the New Testament.

CHAPTER 3

THE SEVENTH DAY VIEW

The Sabbath in the Teaching of Christ

All portions of Scripture concerning the nature of the Sabbath are important, but of special interest are the portions of Scripture which indicate Christ's attitude and view of the Sabbath. In this chapter Bacchiocchi's conviction of the view of Christ will be presented.

Luke 4

It is obvious that Christ claims in the New Testament to be the fulfillment of the Old Testament Messianic promises. But Bacchiacchi not only believes He is the fulfillment of the Messianic promises, but also the fulfillment of the Sabbatical promises of salvation.

When Christ came to His hometown of Nazareth and read the Isaiah passage in the synagogue, He proclaimed the acceptable year of the Lord as described in that passage. These are Sabbatical promises which He read, including healing for the broken-hearted, deliverance to the captives, and liberty for the oppressed. This is Jubilee year terminology and stresses that the liberty and redemptive implications of the Jubilee and Sabbath year are now made available in the Messiah.[1]

Even if that be the case, a key question arises here. Having seen that Christ makes available the redemption and liberation promised by the Jubilee and annual Sabbath years, does He also make available the redemption and liberation of the weekly Sabbath? Bacchiocchi says the answer must be yes. If one asks why, the answer must be two-fold. First, because of the close connection between the annual and weekly Sabbaths. Second, it is also because of the "today" of Luke 4. Jesus said, "Today is this scripture fulfilled in your ears." That "today," though having a broader scope, refers primarily to the actual Sabbath on which Jesus spoke.[2] Thus it is clear to Bacchiocchi that the coming of Christ represents the fulfillment of God's purposes for this world as expressed initially through the blessing and the sanctification of the Sabbath at creation.[3] In simple words, Christ is the fulfillment of the Sabbath promise which was given at creation, and the blessings which He brings are also the fulfillment of the Sabbath promises.

Sabbath Controversies

Bacchiocchi's claim that Christ was the fulfillment of the Messianic expectations inherent in the Sabbath raises some vital questions. For example, how did Christ Himself view the subject, especially the actual observance of the Sabbath? Did He teach that the Sabbath institution and Sabbath observance was the unquestionable will of God for His followers? Or did Christ regard the obligation of Sabbath-keeping as fulfilled, superseded and therefore set aside with His coming?[4]

The answers to these questions are found, according to Bacchiocchi, in the Sabbath controversies as recorded in the Gospels. It is true that post-exilic Judaism erected a fence around the Sabbath turning the day into a legalistic ritual rather than a day of loving service. This is the reason the Sabbath controversies arose between Christ and the Jewish leaders of His day. Christ was not in conflict to the true Old Testament teaching on the Sabbath, but he was in direct conflict with post-exilic Judaism's view of the Sabbath, especially as it was reflected in the rabbinic regulations. Just as Christ restored to the law its original intent in the Sermon on the Mount, even so He had to liberate the Sabbath commandment from its perversions.[5]

The Disciples Plucking Grain

In the incident of the disciples plucking grain on the Sabbath (Mark 2 and Matthew 12), Christ refers to David's eating the shewbread and the priests of the Old Testament working on the Sabbath. Both actions were unlawful.

Nevertheless, David's action was blameless because mercy is more important than sacrifice. And the priests who worked on the Sabbath were also innocent because of the redemptive nature of their work.

From this basis it can be shown on several counts that the disciples of Christ are also innocent in their plucking grain on the Sabbath. For one thing, as Matthew 12:6 declares, One greater than the temple is present. For another, Christ fulfils His ministry of salvation on behalf of the needy as the true High Priest.[6] But it must be understood that this passage gives no sanction to any idea that Christ set aside the Sabbath. Rather He sought to set forth its true interpretation and its proper place for His people.

Healing on the Sabbath

The same is true of Christ's healing on the Sabbath in Matthew 12:9-14, says Bacchiocchi. That is to say again, Christ is not opposing the Sabbath, but He is demonstrating that the Sabbath was to be observed as a day of redemption and of experiencing the blessing of salvation.[7] The Sabbath was instituted to contribute to and to ensure man's well-being, and a denial of the meeting of human needs on the Sabbath would be a violation and prevention of its original purpose.[8] Christ and His disciples in this passage, therefore, are not setting the Sabbath aside, but neither are they guilty of breaking the Sabbath. They are innocent, not because of some supposed authority Christ had to transcend the law, but because their actions fell within the intent of the law itself.[9]

The Lord of the Sabbath

The statement by Christ in Mark 2:27-28 that He is the Lord of the Sabbath further underscores the function of the Sabbath, contends Bacchiocchi. Christ's intent in this passage is not to argue the universal scope of the Sabbath in opposition to the Palestinian view that the Sabbath was for Jews only (though Christ no doubt took the universal view).

Neither is Christ saying that the well-being and comfort of humanity is more important than Sabbath rest, as if the Sabbath restricted man's welfare and comfort. Christ says that the Sabbath was made because of man. It was not given to make people slaves of rules and regulations, but to ensure physical and spiritual well-being. Therefore, proper Sabbath observance does not restrict or damage our welfare, but it guarantees it. Christ's Lordship over the Sabbath represents His authority over humanity and His authority to determine how the Sabbath should be kept.[10]

Therefore, again the Lord of the Sabbath statements confirm Sabbath observance and give guidance as to its purpose, rather than setting it aside.

John 5:1-18

In this passage the Pharisees charge that Christ cannot be from God because He supposedly broke the Sabbath when He healed a man and then told him to carry his pallet (5:10 and 16). Jesus responded in verse 17 saying, "My Father is working still and I am working." Bacchiocchi says that the phrase "working still" should not be seen as a reference to the work of creation as as if God had been in a continual act of creating since creation. Such an interpretation would nullify Sabbath observance.[11] Any interpretation which suggests that Christ was announcing through His Sabbath deeds even in a veiled manner the end of Sabbath observance is to be rejected. This is the same accusation the Jews leveled at Christ when they accused Him of breaking the Sabbath.

The phrase "working still" then does not refer to creation but to the redemptive acts of God and Christ. Christ denies the charge of breaking the Sabbath by arguing that His works of salvation are not excluded but they are the works expected by the Sabbath commandment.[12] Although it is true that we should do the works of God everyday (John 9:14), the Sabbath is the time we can best fulfill our ministry since on that day we commemorate the "working still" of God.[13]

The conclusion of this passage, therefore, and all the passages which have been considered in the Sabbath controversies, is that they affirm that Christ did not come to do away with the Sabbath, but to restore it to its proper function. Christ's attitude toward the Sabbath must be seen in the context of His overall attitude toward the law. by doing good and healing on the Sabbath He showed its true function.

Questions and Conclusions Arising from the Sabbath Controversy Narratives

The discussion of this chapter leads to some important questions and conclusions concerning the Sabbath.

First, the redemptive nature of the Sabbath confirmed by Christ shows its permanence. If healing on the Sabbath was evidence of the presence and blessing of Christ's redemption, does it not seem improper to choose a different day, such as Sunday, to worship the Redeemer? Rather does not Christ make the day a fitting and permanent memorial of the reality of His redemptive mission by His fulfilling the redemptive purpose of the Sabbath?[14]

Second, since Christ never hints at the possibility of an eventual replacement of the Sabbath, but rather fully confirms it, why would He wish to change the day? What new benefit would there be in changing the day of worship?[15]

Third, Christ's commandments establish the permanence of the Sabbath. Did not Christ also take for granted the permanence of the Sabbath after His departure by His commandments in Matthew 24:20 concerning "fleeing" on the Sabbath? Is not this matter of "fleeing" an action which will take place after Christ has died and risen? And does this not imply that Christ does not foresee its substitution with another day of worship? Is it not clear also that the Sabbath was still observed by the Jewish Christians when Matthew wrote his gospel?[16]

Fourth, the Sabbath conflict narratives affirm the permanence of the Sabbath. These narratives, which center on the manner of Sabbath observance, are indicative of the high estimate of the Sabbath in Jewish circles and even in primitive Christianity.[17] If the gospel writers were already observing Sunday rather than the Jewish Sabbath, why would they report so many Sabbath healings of Jesus? Their concern over Christ's Sabbath activities and teaching hardly suggests they were observing Sunday.[18]

Conclusion

The teaching of Christ concerning the Sabbath is undeniable for Bacchiocchi. Christ's intent was to re-establish the Sabbath day according to its proper function and purpose, which would include the worship of God on that day according to the fourth commandment. There is no evidence in His teachings nor is there any example in His actions that He meant to establish another day besides Saturday as the proper day for worship and Sabbath observance.

CHAPTER 4

THE SEVENTH DAY VIEW

The Sabbath Rest of Hebrews

No view of the Sabbath is complete without the consideration of the concept of Sabbath rest in the book of Hebrews. Bacchiocchi does not by-pass this section of Scripture in his presentation and argumentation.

Sabbath Rest Today

The book of Hebrews, says Bacchiocchi, was written to a group of Jewish believers who were convinced that the blessings of Sabbath-keeping were connected to the Jewish national covenant. These Jewish believers also were convinced that Sabbath observance was associated with earthly material prosperity which only members of the Jewish community would enjoy in a state of political peace.

Hebrews 4 refutes this idea. The author wants to wean them away from a limited and material view of the Sabbath and to establish its universal, redemptive and spiritual nature. This is accomplished as the writer of Hebrews quotes both Genesis 2 and Psalms 95.[1]

By quoting Genesis 2, which states "And He rested on the seventh day from all His work," the author traces the origin of Sabbath-rest back to the time of creation. The fact that the Sabbath originated with God at creation gives it universal and eternal validity.[2]

Psalms 95:7-8 also shows the universal and redemptive scope of Sabbath rest. The challenge in these verses is "Today if you will hear his voice, harden not your heart." Thus the Sabbath rest still needs to be entered (Hebrews 4:6) since it is the conviction of the writer of Hebrews that it was not entered by the wilderness generation. Further, God's Sabbath-rest did not end with Joshua, but was available in

David's time. And the "today" has now dawned with the coming of Christ. Now men must enter into Sabbath rest. By using two verses the writer of Hebrews shows that God's people in Christ share in God's purpose of creation and redemption as pictured in the Sabbath. They both speak of entering into Sabbath rest as God rested at creation. Therefore Genesis 2:2, which says God rested the seventh day from all his work, and Psalms 95:11, which declares God swore in his wrath they would not enter his rest, show that God's people through Christ share in the whole purpose of creation and redemption epitomized by Sabbath rest.[3]

Thus Bacchiocchi is convinced that Christ's first coming illuminated the spiritual understanding of Sabbath-keeping in order to wean believers away from an earthly nationalistic understanding of its observance. This also reassured the readers of Hebrews of the permanence of the blessing pictured in Sabbath rest. The nature of these blessings consists of a present salvation rest and a future restoration rest which God offers to believers.[4]

Objections to Bacchiocchi's View

Some have argued that the writer of Hebrews in chapter 4 is not discussing actual Sabbath observance, but the fulfilling of the spiritual blessing connected with Sabbath rest. Therefore, no inference can be drawn from this section of Scripture concerning the literal Sabbath observance.

Bacchiocchi replies that such a conclusion is not justified.[5] The recipients of the letter were so steeped in and attracted to Jewish liturgy that it was unnecessary to encourage actual Sabbath observance.[6] They did not need to hear about the binding nature of the Sabbath commandments, but they did need to hear its true meaning in light of the coming of Christ.[7] In simple words, just because the author of Hebrews does not mention literal Sabbath observance, that does not mean he did not have it in view. He explained the spiritual meaning of the Sabbath without unnecessarily reminding Sabbath-observing Jews of their responsibility.

Bacchiocchi continues his argumentation by declaring there are several factors in Hebrews 4 which indicate it is speaking of a present Sabbath-keeping experience. In verse 3 the verb is a present tense and can be translated "for we who have believed are entering into rest." Thus it speaks of an entering into rest now and does not restrict it to a future hour only.

A second factor which indicates these verses speak of a present experience of Sabbath-keeping is the verb "remains" in 4:6 and 9. Literally it means "to be left behind." It is a present passive and does not necessarily imply a future prospect either. These verses could be translated "It is left behind that some must enter into it . . . " (verse 6), and "there is left behind, therefore, a rest to the people of God" (verse 9). Obviously, this does remove it from a future prospect.

A third factor which pushes the verse towards a present experience of Sabbath-keeping is the word "today."[8] Bacchiocchi might well ask how "today" could be construed as speaking of tomorrow.

A fourth factor indicating this is a present day experience of Sabbath-keeping is the word "sabbatismas" in 4:9. This word refers to the rest of the seventh day and not the rest in some future day. The verb "sabbatizo" is used in the Greek Old Testament (the Septuagint) in Exodus 16:30, Leviticus 23:32 and 2 Chronicles 36:21 to refer to Sabbath observance.[9]

Finally, a fifth factor indicates that Hebrews 4 speaks of a present day Sabbath-keeping experience. Bacchiocchi cites the comparison between God entering His rest and ceasing from His works and the believer entering rest and ceasing from his works. The comparison is not about a future rest in death for the verbs are aorist (past tense) and not future.[10] Further, the comparison is not about works themselves, since God's works are good and ours are evil. But the comparison has to do with our imitation of God resting from works. The author of Hebrews explains the nature of Sabbath rest by referring to its basic characteristic, which is cessation from work. The act of resting on the Sabbath represents the stopping of one's doing in order to experience being saved by faith. There is opportunity every week on the Sabbath to enter God's rest, which in turn anticipates the final redemption that the Sabbath itself represents.[11]

Summary

In summary, Bacchiocchi sees Hebrews 4 as a refutation of the idea that the blessings of Sabbath-keeping were tied to the Jewish national covenant. The author traces the origin of Sabbath rest back to creation. Yet the Sabbath also possesses, according to Hebrews 4, a universal and redemptive scope. Sabbath rest can and must be entered now. That Sabbath rest available now is the salvation rest which will eventually include a future restoration rest. All of this is anchored and figured in actual Sabbath observances and it is not just the fulfillment of future Sabbath blessings.

CHAPTER 5

THE SEVENTH DAY VIEW

The Sabbath
in the Teachings of Paul

The question to be faced at this juncture is, what is Paul's view of the Sabbath? Is there any evidence that he encouraged or taught that the Sabbath would be abolished? Or is there any evidence that Paul ever sought to introduce Sunday worship? Paul's view, as seen by Bacchiocchi, will be presented in this chapter.

Paul's View

Bacchiocchi is convinced that there is absolutely no evidence that Paul ever taught an elimination of the Sabbath or the introduction of Sunday worship. He says that as long as a principle was not involved, Paul showed an unwillingness to offend his Jewish brethren in matters of the law. He reassured the Jews in Acts 24:17-18 concerning his respect for the law. Why should we believe then that Paul would offend the Jews by any such attempt to change the day of worship from the seventh day of the week to the first day, especially when there is no evidence whatsoever?[1]

Problem Texts

Bacchiocchi acknowledges there are three key passages in Paul's writings which have been used to argue that Paul no longer held the Sabbath to be binding, especially for Gentile Christians. These texts are Colossians 2:14-17, Galatians 4:8-11 and Romans 14:5-6.[2] He discusses each of them in detail.

Colossians 2:14-17

This section of Scripture has been interpreted to mean that the Sabbath is a Jewish institution which was abolished by Christ on the cross.[3] These verses read as follows:

14) Blotting out the handwriting of ordinances
that was against us, which was contrary to
us, and took it out of the way, nailing it to
his cross;
15) And having spoiled principalities and powers,
he made a show of them openly, triumphing
over them in it.
16) Let no man, therefore, judge you in meat,
or in drink, or in respect of an holy day,
or of the new moon or of the Sabbath days,
17) which are a shadow of things to come; but
the body is of Christ.

The key points stated in these verses are:

1. that Christ blotted out the handwriting of
ordinances (requirements) that was against
us (verse 14).

2. that, therefore, we should not be judged in regard
to Sabbaths (verse 16).

3. that such things are a shadow of things to come
(verse 17).

Obviously each of these needs careful examination.

First, what does Paul mean by the "handwriting of ordinances (requirements) that was against us?" If this phrase does refer to the Mosaic law and its ordinances, as some would want to interpret it, then there exists a legitimate possibility that the Sabbath could be included in the ordinances nailed to the cross. However, Bacchiocchi argues that the word for handwriting (cheirographon) means either a "certificate of indebtedness" resulting from our transgressions, or a "book containing the record of sins" used for the condemnation of mankind. The word, he says, does not refer to the law of Moses, since the law was not a book of records. What God destroyed on the cross was not the legal ground for our entanglement into sin, that is the law, but God destroyed on the cross the written record of our sins.[4] Therefore, if this phrase does not mean that God destroyed the law, then it cannot mean that he destroyed the Sabbath requirement of the law.

Second, in understanding this passage in Colossians, one must ask what Paul is referring to in verse 16 when he mentions allowing no man to judge you concerning "a holy day or new moon or Sabbath." Bacchiocchi says these do refer to annual, monthly, and weekly observances of the Old Testament so that the Sabbath day is included.[5] However, it is important, he says, to ask whether these regulations belong exclusively to the Mosaic law.[6]

At this point, Bacchiocchi feels an understanding of the Colossian heresy is important. The false teaching in Colossae, though difficult to define, seems to be characterized by a theological and practical error. The theological error included a denial of the supremacy of Christ by the worship of the elements of the universe. The source of authority became man-made tradition. The practical error, on the other hand, consisted of a strict asceticism and ritualism.[7] The practices of special days came from the Old Testament, but the part which had been united with the practices were foreign to the Old Testament. The Colossian heresy is based on this perversion of Old Testament practices and not Jewish legalism. This explains why the word "law" is absent in the discussion.[8] Therefore it is legitimate to ask whether this passage should be used to define Paul's basic attitude towards the Sabbath.[9]

In simple words, since Paul in the book of Colossians is dealing with a serious theological perversion of the supremacy of Christ and a serious practical perversion of proper living and worship practices, even a perversion which is not based on Jewish legalism, it is not correct to define Paul's basic attitude towards the Sabbath from these verses. The point Bacchiocchi wants to make is this: what is said about a distorted use of an institution like the Sabbath, cannot be used to challenge the validity of the commandment itself. A precept is not nullified by the condemnation of its abuse.[10]

Third, what is to be made of the phrase stating that these things are a "shadow" of things to come? Bacchiocchi says that Paul places these practices in their proper perspective with Christ in this contrast. Both verbs in verse 17 are present tense ("are" a shadow of things to come and the body "is" of Christ). It does not say they were shadows. This shows these practices have a legitimate function even after the first coming of Christ.

Further, the term "shadow" is not a negative label for worthless observances which have ceased their function. Rather the term is a fitting symbol of the present and future blessing of salvation.   Even dietary scruples and the observance of holy days can serve as a shadow preparing Christians for the world to come.[11]

Thus Bacchiocchi sees no ground in the Colossians passage for arguing that Paul believed and taught that Sabbath observance was abolished for believers today.

Romans 14

The problem in Romans 14 centers on Paul's discussion about believers not judging each other concerning differing opinions about eating practices and observances of days. Bacchiocchi says this passage is no problem at all for it is only remotely, if at all, related to the Mosaic law.

Concerning the eating practices, he says that the Old Testament does not prescribe a strict vegetarianism, nor a total abstinence from wine, nor a preference for fasting days, which practices were the subject of Romans 14. Besides that, the Sabbath was not a fasting day, but a day of feasting. Therefore the comments Paul makes on eating practices could not refer to the Sabbath.

But what about the reference to Paul's comments on the observance of days? Again, here in Romans, it is not the law that is in view, but ascetic beliefs derived from sectarian

Judaism that Paul has in mind.[12] Therefore the statements about observances of days in Romans 14 cannot be applied to Sabbath observance.

Galatians 4:9-10

In Galatians 4:9-10 Paul equates the observance of days and months and seasons and years with turning again to the weak and beggarly elements which brings bondage. The text declares:

9) But now, after that you have known God, or rather are known by God, how turn you again to the weak and beggarly elements unto which you desire again to be in bondage?
10) You observe days, and months, and times, and years.

Bacchiocchi is not convinced any of these categories have anything to do in negating proper Sabbath-keeping. The "days" could include a reference to the Sabbath because of the parallel with Colossians 2:16. But it must be understood that the Galatians, rather than being properly motivated to keep the Jewish festivals, were doing so because of superstitious beliefs in astral influences, that is influences relating to the stars (4:8-9). Paul is challenging a whole system of salvation as presented by the false teachers. This false motivation for observing days and seasons undermined the gospel. Therefore Paul is not opposing the principle of Sabbath-keeping, but the perverted use of worship observances.[13] Thus the apostle is not lashing out against the form of these observances, but the perverted function.

Bacchiocchi says further that whether or not a Christian eats, drinks and observes days is a matter of personal conviction, but the reason for observing these practices is not a matter of personal viewpoint.[14] They should not be done for self-righteous purposes.[15]

Conclusion

In conclusion, according to Bacchiocchi, there is nothing in the epistles of Paul that indicates he taught or encouraged an elimination of the Sabbath or the introduction of the first day as the day of worship. Therefore, one would conclude that Paul agreed with a continuing and permanent Sabbath observance even for the New Testament believer.

CHAPTER 6

THE SEVENTH DAY VIEW

The Sabbath and Sunday in the Post-Apostolic Church

One of the problems of the Seventh Day view is to explain what caused the church in its history to abandon the strong and prominent Jewish tradition of Sabbath-keeping in favor of a new day of worship, the first day of the week. After all, were not the Jewish practices, including the Sabbath, a very central part of Jewish life, and was not the early church strongly Jewish? How could such a change take place if there was not some divine reason for it?

Bacchiocchi feels that attention must be given to a great number of contributing factors and influences, including theological, social, political and even pagan. All of these may have had a role in the adoption of Sunday as the day of worship, even without divine sanction.[1] Following are some of his arguments.

Sunday Worship Did Not Arise in the Jerusalem Church

The early church, which was centered in Jerusalem, was made up mostly of Jewish converts and ex-priests (Acts 6:7 and 21:30). Understandably, these Jewish converts would have continued the religious practices that they were accustomed to observing. Thus the early Jerusalem church would have had a distinct Jewish theological conviction which would also have reflected Jewish practices.[2] The meeting places mentioned most frequently in Acts are the Temple, the synagogue, and private homes. These gatherings in homes, says Bacchiocchi, were not seen as conflicting with the services in the Temple or synagogue, but were understood to be complimenting them.

Clearly then, early Christian worship arose not as a new institution, but as a continuation and reinterpretation of Jewish religious services. Thus the earliest Christians at first looked like a party within Judaism.[3] Therefore, because of this strong Jewish composition of the Jerusalem church, it would have been almost impossible for any church anywhere to introduce Sunday observance prior to 70 A.D.[4]

What then about the destruction of Jerusalem in 70 A.D.? Could this event have brought with it factors which moved the day of worship from the seventh to the first day of the week? Bacchiocchi admits that the destruction of Jerusalem did have decisive effects on the relation between Judaism and Christianity, but he is not convinced that this event of the fall of Jerusalem provided the break of Palestinian Christianity with Sabbath-keeping. Both Eusebius (260-340 A.D.) and Epiphanius (315-403 A.D.) wrote that the church in Jerusalem up to Hadrian's siege (135 A.D.) consisted of converted Jewish people. Thus their basic attitude would have been deep loyalty to Jewish customs.[5]

Important to the discussion also, Bacchiocchi argues, is a curse which was introduced into the synagogue services around 80-90 A.D. to detect the presence of Christians who were in attendance.[6] This shows that as late as the first century many Jewish Christians in Palestine considered themselves to be Jews and they attended Sabbath services in the synagogue. Therefore Jewish Christians could not have been responsible for the substitution of Sunday worship for Sabbath-keeping. In fact, Sunday worship could not have arisen in Jerusalem before 135 A.D.[7]

Sunday Worship Arose
in a Community of Gentile Believers

Where and how, then, did Sunday worship originate? Bacchiocchi contends that the most likely place to look would be in those churches which were predominantly Gentile--churches which had no previous ties even with Judaism, and perhaps churches which were even in conflict with Judaism. Such a setting would allow for the substitution of Christian practices for the Jewish ones. For these new practices to gain widespread approval, it would require also an ecclesiastical power that already had gained wide recognition. On this basis, Bacchiocchi nominates the city of Rome as the place where Sunday observance had its birthplace.[8]

No doubt, according to Bacchiocchi, the Christian community of Rome was made up of a majority of Gentile believers (see Romans 11 and 13) along with a Jewish minority (see Romans 14). Emperor Claudius in 49 A.D. had expelled the Jews from Rome, including Christian Jews. Fourteen years later Nero identified the Christians as a separate entity from the Jews in his persecution of the Christians. This differentiation seems to be a natural result of the attempts made by both Jews and Gentiles to distinguish themselves from each other. The abandonment of the Sabbath and the adoption of Sunday as a day of worship may have occurred in Rome as a part of this process of Christians separating themselves from Judaism.[9]

Anti-Jewish feelings and anti-Jewish riots erupted among the Romans after Nero in 66-70 A.D. and later in 132-135 A.D. Many times Christians suffered also in these anti-Jewish outbreaks even though they were not Jews. The reason was that Christians were not seen as defenders of Roman religion for they were converting more pagans to Christianity than the Jews were to Judaism.

The Roman government also began to react militarily, financially, and religiously against the Jews and their religious observances, especially circumcision and the Sabbath.[10] Because of these hostile attitudes and actions against the Jews, the church of Rome assumed an attitude of reconciliation towards the Roman government, and they also adopted an attitude and practice of radical separation from the Jews and Jewish practices. Obviously these circumstances invited Christians to develop a new identity characterized by a negative attitude towards the Jews and their religious practices, which also brought a substitution of new religious customs and observances for the old Jewish ones.[11]

The Second Century Fathers
Wrote against Sabbath-Keeping

It is clear that the early church fathers of the second century wrote against Sabbath-keeping. Ignatius in Asia Minor (100 A.D.), Barnabas in Alexandria (135 A.D.) and Justin Martyr, who taught and wrote in Rome in the middle of the second century, all denounced Sabbath-keeping. Justin provides the most devastating and systematic condemnation of the Sabbath and the first explicit account of Sunday worship. The question is why these church fathers rejected the keeping of the Sabbath.

Justin saw the Sabbath as a temporary ordinance derived from Moses. To him it was an ordinance which God did not intend man to keep literally since God Himself does not stop controlling the universe on the seventh day of creation.[12] Justin also argued in favor of Sunday observance because light was created on the first day, because the resurrection of Christ was on the first day, and because circumcision took place on the eighth day.[13]

Bacchiocchi feels some of these arguments, which are used to justify and exalt Sunday at the expense of the Sabbath, are controversial and even absurd, and thus support his own view. Bacchioicchi's own view is that Sunday observance was introduced into a climate of controversy where the church was trying to make a break with Judaism.[14] Such an action did not have divine direction or sanction.

Conclusion

Bacchiocchi is convinced there is no historical evidence that the early church adopted Sunday as the day of worship on any proper divinely sanctioned grounds. It was purely a move brought about by other factors--not by God's intent nor direction. Clearly to his understanding, Sunday observance does not rest on a foundation of Biblical theology or apostolic authority, but rather on the ecclesiastical efforts of the second century church.[15]

CHAPTER 7

THE SEVENTH DAY VIEW

Practical Considerations

Bacchiocchi is convinced that there is a real need for Sabbath rest in our society today. He points out that the radical transformation which has taken place in our society today because of technological, industrial and scientific achievements has led to a greater availability of leisure time and money. The result of this is that there is a temptation to consider this time as our own by using it for self-gratification, while rationalizing away our obligation to observe the Sabbath.[1]

Part of the crisis surrounding the need for Sabbath rest has to do with our views of the Sabbath commandment, Bacchiocchi continues to argue. He says it is difficult to make Sunday carry the weight of the theology of the Sabbath because Sunday worship arose from church tradition and not from Biblical precepts. In fact, he maintains, it is virtually impossible to construct a valid theological basis to require rest on Sunday.

Some solve this problem by divorcing worship from rest and view Sunday as the <u>hour</u> of worship.[2] However, Bacchiocchi is convinced that to divorce worship from rest is to misunderstand the meaning of the Sabbath commandment, which ordains the consecration of the day to the Lord, not just one <u>hour</u>.[3] What is needed is a Sabbath proposal which could revitalize both worship and rest. Bacchiocchi says the Christian community needs to be educated to understand and experience the Biblical and apostolic meaning and obligation to the seventh day Sabbath. There needs to be a rediscovery and a restoration of those permanent categories established by Scripture which make the Sabbath God's holy day for the Christian today.[4]

What Is Sabbath Rest?

Resting on the Sabbath does involve abstaining from work, but it is more than just inactivity or self-centered physical relaxation.[5] Neither is it merely waiting for the hours to pass away so a person then can resume some kind of meaningful activity.[6] The physical rest is to be divinely centered rest which not only brings physical rest, but also enables a person to become free for God and others. Resting on the Sabbath is holy to the Lord and is an expression of our complete commitment to Him. Such rest itself is an act of worship.[7]

What Are the Practical Benefits of Sabbath Rest?

Sabbath rest has many practical benefits, according to Bacchiocchi. Some of these are as follows.

First, Sabbath rest gives a sense of completeness to our life and work which is incomplete. By resting on the Sabbath we celebrate the completion and perfection of creation as if all our work were done. It is impossible to praise God for His marvelous accomplishments if we are living under a deep sense of personal failure and frustration because our work is not done. But by resting on the Sabbath we are given a sense of completeness which in turn gives meaning and direction to our lives.[8]

Second, Sabbath rest provides an opportunity to worship God in a joyful celebration. Those who say they find the Sabbath depressing have accepted Sabbath time but do not know or live in light of the Sabbath good news. They center on the bad news of what cannot be done, instead of the good news of things to be enjoyed.[9] Clearly, the Sabbath should be a joyful time of celebration because of the good news. It should be a time of worship as well. Some seek to argue against the Sabbath as a day of worship by saying that every day is a day of worship and thereby is a Sabbath, but such ideas result in no Sabbath at all and even no worship at all offered to God.[10] Bacchiocchi admits that worship can be offered to God on any day, but the Sabbath day provides a special day of worship because God has promised His sanctifying presence in a special way on the Sabbath. Third, Sabbath rest provides a special way to experience God's revelation. This experience of God's revelation is both individual and collective in public and communal worship.[11]

Fourth, Sabbath rest gives an individual the opportunity to serve God by helping others. Serving God by helping others allows the Sabbath to become a remedy for any possibility of one worshipping his work or his leisure.[12]

Fifth, Sabbath rest helps people to have time and opportunity to re-order their priorities. This re-ordering of priorities will bring renewal, order and harmony into the fragmented lives of people.[13]

Sixth, the Sabbath may have something to say to us concerning ecological crisis. The Sabbath is a memorial of an originally perfect creation and as such assures us that God created the world good. But the world is no longer a perfect creation, nor does man respect the creation as he should. But the Sabbath does encourage respect for the creation by reminding us that we share with nature the goal of ultimate restoration. Further, besides having theological implications of the necessity to respect the creation, the Sabbath provides valuable opportunities to translate into action the theological values of stewardship of the creation.[14] Sabbath-keeping in the sense of resting one day in seven acknowledges God's authority of the world and implies our responsibility as caretakers of His creation. A Sabbath lifestyle does not exploit creation, but admires and cares for it.[15]

Conclusion

Thus Bacchiocchi is convinced that the Sabbath is needed today for various practical reasons. It gives a completeness to life, provides man an opportunity to worship, provides man an opportunity to experience God's revelation, gives an opportunity to serve God by helping others, gives opportunity to re-order priorities, and speaks to man concerning ecological matters. Sabbath observance nourishes a three-dimensional faith, that is, a faith which ties together three necessary elements--the theme of creation, the theme of redemption, and the theme of final restoration. It lays the foundation for a faith which recognizes and reacts properly to creation, which helps man keep a proper perspective of the past, present, and future.[16]

CHAPTER 8

THE SEVENTH DAY VIEW

The Rebuttal of Arguments for Sunday Worship

Bacchiocchi is aware that his view is often rejected because of several common arguments given in favor of Sunday worship. He seeks to refute them with counter arguments.

Objection One:
The First Day Is the Day
Christ Rose from the Dead

One of the most common and popular arguments for worshipping on Sunday is because this is the day Christ rose from the dead. Bacchiocchi admits that there is no doubt that the New Testament places an incomparable importance on the event of the resurrection. However, there is no indication that there should be a special day of worship to commemorate it. The resurrection could be celebrated monthly or annually.[1] Sunday observance is not tied to the resurrection in the early church of the first or second century. It was not until Augustine in the fifth century that the resurrection was made a reason for Sunday observance.[2]

Further, not only is Sunday observance never tied to the resurrection in the Bible or the early church, but the concept of Sabbath rest is never tied to any important event of Christ's life.

Bacchiocchi maintains that such subjective reasoning of tying the day of worship to an important event of Christ's life could be used to justify the worthiness of Thursday or even Friday for important events which took place on those days as well. The truth is that believers are to honor the resurrection, not by Sunday observance, but by walking in newness of life (see Romans 6:4 and Colossians 2:12-13).[3]

But even if one does want to establish a day as the day of worship because of an event on that day or because of the importance of that day, one can argue for the Sabbath as the day of worship. It has already been shown that the Sabbath was the symbol of Christ's redemptive mission.

To repeat Bacchiocchi's argument, he notes that it was on a Friday afternoon that Christ completed His redemptive mission on earth. He cried, "It is finished." He then hallowed the Sabbath by resting in the tomb. Just as the Sabbath rest at the end of creation expressed the joy and satisfaction of God over a complete and perfect creation, so the Sabbath rest at the end of Christ's ministry expressed the rejoicing of God over a complete and perfect redemption restored to man.[4] Why not then worship on the Sabbath since it is a symbol of this redemptive mission fulfilled by Christ, and since the Sabbath day at the end of His life completed that redemptive mission?[5]

Objection Two: The First Day Is the Day Christ Appeared to His Apostles

The second argument in favor of worship on the first day is that this is the day Christ appeared to His apostles after His resurrection. But according to Bacchiocchi these appearances of Christ to His apostles are hardly substantial enough to justify a new day of worship.

In Luke 24:21 and John 20:19 the disciples gathered on the first day of the week out of fear and not from any kind of celebration.

John 21:3 says that the disciples went fishing all night, probably after observing the Sabbath.

Again, John 20:26 does not suggest a regular pattern of Sunday observance, but the gathering on the first day is mentioned because Thomas was not present on the previous appearance (see verse 24).

Thus the appearances of Christ do not follow a consistent pattern and therefore cannot be used to justify a recurring celebration on Sunday.[6]

Objection Three:
Sunday Is the Day of Worship
Because of Apostolic Example

Three passages are used to argue apostolic example or even apostolic command for Sunday worship. They are Acts 20:7, 1 Corinthians 16:2 and Revelation 1:10. All three will be discussed here in the presentation of Bacchiocchi's view.

Acts 20:7

Acts 20:7 is seen by many as clear evidence that the early church worshipped on the first day of the week in a continuing and habitual manner. The verse reads, "On the first day of the week when the disciples came together to break bread, Paul preached unto them, ready to depart on the next day, and continued his speech until midnight."

Bacchiocchi raises several questions about this passage. First, if Luke is using the Roman method of computing time (a day begins at midnight), then this is Sunday evening. However, the breaking of bread did not take place until after midnight, which would make it Monday.[7] It is more likely that Luke is using the Jewish method of computing time (a day begins at sunset) for he consistently uses the Jewish method. If so, the gathering then takes place on Saturday evening, which makes it unlikely that it was a formal and regular Sunday service.[8]

In either case, whether this service took place on a Saturday or Sunday night is not the key issue. The more important factor is that it was not an ordinary meeting, but a special gathering occasioned by the departure of the apostle Paul. And the fact that the breaking of bread occurred late (after midnight), when believers were hardly awake, suggests that its function was more social than religious.[9] Luke mentions the day of the meeting because Paul is about ready to depart, and the raising of Eutychus is an extra-ordinary miracle which produces an additional chronological reference to describe the unfolding of Paul's journey.[10]

1 Corinthians 16:1-2

This passage states, "Now concerning the collection for the saints, as I have given order to the churches of Galatia, even so do ye. Upon the first day of the week let every one of you lay by him in store, as God has prospered him, that there be no gathering when I come."

Bacchiocchi is convinced these instructions given by Paul have nothing to do with regular habitual weekly worship, but rather they are to guarantee that an efficient collection is in place upon his arrival. The collection was to be periodical--the first day of the week. It was to be personal as the command is to "each one of you." It was to be private as each one was to "lay by in store." And it was to be proportional--in accordance as each has prospered.'

Thus the first day of the week here was strictly practical rather than theological. No financial transactions were performed by the Jews on the Sabbath. So it is understandable that this money would be laid aside on another day, even preferably the first day of the week before it was used for other purposes.[11] Clearly nothing in this passage suggests a public assembly. The stress is laid on what one would do individually, privately and at home.[12]

Revelation 1:10

The phrase "the Lord's Day" in Revelation 1:10 is used to argue apostolic example of Sunday worship. But Bacchiocchi is not convinced that the phrase refers to Sunday. He contends that the equation of Sunday with the Lord's Day is not based on internal evidence in the book of Revelation nor from the remainder of the New Testament. Rather, he says, it is based on writings from the latter part of the second century.[13] In the apocryphal <u>Gospel of Peter</u> the phrase "the Lord's Day" occurs twice as a translation of "the first day of the week" in Mark 16:2.[14] The major question, however, is whether Sunday was designated as "the Lord's Day" by the end of the first century when the book of Revelation was written.[15]

It is clear that in the New Testament Sunday is always called the first day of the week. Then the question becomes, when looking at Revelation 1:10, why John would use the phrase "the Lord's Day" to refer to Sunday? Why did he not use the term "first day?" And further, if John wrote the book of Revelation and his gospel at the same time (near the end of the first century), why does not the phrase "the Lord's Day" appear in the gospel of John? If a new designation ("the Lord's Day") that expressed the meaning and nature of Christian worship was already in use, a Christian writer could hardly legitimately continue to use the Jewish designation ("the first day of the week") instead.[16]

Therefore, on these stated grounds, the phrase "the Lord's Day" could not refer to Sunday. Then what does it refer to? Bacchiocchi answers that it refers to the eschatological day of the Lord. The immediate context in Revelation, he says, refers unmistakably to the eschatological day of the Lord (verse 7 mentions Christ's second coming).

His second coming constitutes the focal point of every vision in the book and is the theme around which the book of Revelation revolves. John in 1:10 is transported to the future glorious day of the Lord.[17] This is not a reference to Sunday.

Objection Four:
Sunday Is the Day of Worship
Because of a Distinction
Between the Ceremonial and Moral Law

The justification of Sunday observance on the basis of a distinction between moral and ceremonial law, for Bacchiocchi, raises some serious questions.[18] How can the Sabbath commandment in the Ten Commandments be both ceremonial and moral? Some seem to contend it is ceremonial in that it specifies the seventh day, but it is moral for setting apart a day of rest for worship. But if one rejects the seventh day Sabbath as the day of worship because it is supposedly ceremonial, does that not also destroy the moral basis for worshipping God on one day at all?[19]

Further, how is it possible to maintain that the Sabbath has been fulfilled and abolished in Jesus[20] and yet argue to practice Sunday observance by appealing to the Sabbath commandment? Again, how can the Sabbath commandment be applied to Sunday when it is the seventh day and not the first day of the week that the commandment declares to keep holy?[21]

Conclusion

Obviously for Bacchiocchi the arguments for Sunday worship raise too many unanswerable questions. All the major passages used by his opponents to argue Sunday worship, if interpreted accurately, he is convinced, fail to establish the case. There are no passages, therefore, in the New Testament which teach by direct command or even by apostolic example that Sunday should be the day of worship for the New Testament church.

PART TWO

THE CHRISTIAN SABBATH VIEW

CHAPTER 9

THE CHRISTIAN SABBATH VIEW

God's Rest at Creation

In part one of this work, the Seventh day view was presented. This position advocates that the Sabbath commandment was permanent and therefore Sabbath observance should be continuing today as it was in the Old Testament.

In this second part a viewpoint which will be called "the Christian Sabbath view" will be set forth. This conviction sees only an indirect connection between the Old Testament Sabbath and our worship practices today. The indirect connection emerges from the belief that, though there is a relation between the Old Testament Sabbath and our practices today, the Sabbath commandment must be seen in light of the changes brought about by the coming of Christ. But these changes do not completely destroy the moral imperative of the Sabbath command for the church for this day--they only alter some factors in the practice of Sabbath observance.

The Sabbath and God's Creation Rest

According to this position the Sabbath is rooted in God's rest at creation. This Sabbath rest will have implications for the new covenant when the Sabbath becomes an eschatological sign pointing to a future Sabbath rest.[1]

After completing the work of creation in six days, Genesis 2:2 states that God rested on the seventh day from all His works. This "rest" of God was not the rest of inactivity, but it was the cessation of the work of creation accompanied by delight in the work which was accomplished.[2] Genesis 2:3 goes on to say that "God blessed the seventh day and sanctified it." That is, God set apart the seventh day. This blessing or setting apart was no doubt for the good of all creation.[3]

Thus God labored six days, rested on the seventh, and blessed and sanctified it for the good of all of His creation. The importance of all of this, especially God's example of working six days and resting the seventh becomes very significant. That example of resting is enough warrant for the believer to observe the day as God did.[4] It would be difficult to understand or explain God's blessing and sanctifying of the seventh day apart from the significance it has for humanity.[5]

John Murray raises several questions to highlight the possible significance of God's example of creation rest for us.[6]

1. Has God's work of creation ceased to be relevant to us?

2. Has the fact that God created in the space of six days and not in one grand action become irrelevant to us?

3. Has the fact that God rested on the seventh day ceased to be relevant to us?

4. Has the divine example become obsolete?

The example of God's rest would have had relevance, it is maintained, for Adam and Eve even before the fall. This period of innocence before man fell should not be seen as an abstract unreal existence. There would have been a concreteness to life in Adam and Eve's paradise and thus also a concreteness to their worship of God. A time for worship would have been needed even before the fall.[7]

The Sabbath As a Creation Ordinance

But does the rest of God at creation have any relationship to the Sabbath of the Mosaic law, or to take the matter even further, to us today? Those who hold to the Christian Sabbath view answer yes to both questions. The reason is that many of this view refer to the Sabbath as a creation ordinance. A creation ordinance can be defined as an ". . . inviable principle inherent in the structure of the world, . . a structural pattern for his creation."[8]

In simple words, it is an unchanging principle for mankind which God established at creation as His purpose and will for mankind. Creation ordinances include the Sabbath, marriage and labor. These creation ordinances are relevant to the very basic nature of man and are an essential part of the activities of humanity.[9]

If one says the Sabbath is a creation ordinance, it follows that the Sabbath possesses a binding nature even before the formal giving of the law at Mt. Sinai. This viewpoint goes on to emphasize that the Sabbath is a part of humanity's "original and constitutional nature" which if set aside would lead to "the moral disorder, degeneracy and degradation of society."[10]

An Argument against the Sabbath As a Creation Ordinance

One possible difficulty with this view, that the Sabbath was constituted as a creation ordinance and that therefore it is to be part of man's life and practice from creation to the present, is the fact that there is no mention of the Sabbath or Sabbath observance before Exodus 16.[11] Gerhardos Vos acknowledges this fact that Exodus 16 is the only mention of Sabbath observance before the giving of the law.[12]

However, this silence, including no mention of patriarchal observance of the Sabbath, is not decisive concerning the issue of a weekly Sabbath as a continuing mandate.[13] It could be explained in a number of ways. Perhaps one possibility was that the observance of the seventh day before Moses was taken for granted as it was also later between Deuteronomy and 2 Kings, and therefore no mention of it needed to be made.[14] Or perhaps it was instituted but not observed just as monogamy was given at creation but then quickly was ignored.[15]

On the positive side there is clear evidence of the seven day week right through the book of Genesis and the early chapters of Exodus.[16] If the seven day week came at creation and not at Mt. Sinai, it is natural to suppose that the Sabbath came with the seven day week.[17] Charles Hodge comments concerning the silence of the Biblical record concerning Sabbath observance before the giving of the law.

> All details not bearing immediately on the design of the author were of necessity left out. If nothing was done but what is there recorded, the antediluvians and patriarchs lived almost entirely without religious observances.[18]

Conclusion

To summarize and conclude this discussion of the Christian Sabbath position, it must be noted that according to this view the Sabbath is a creation ordinance. Though not spelled out explicitly by direct command to be a creation ordinance, there is enough evidence that would lead to that conclusion. That evidence would include God's creation rest and the presence of a seven day week in the history of man. The silence concerning Sabbath observance before Moses does not confine the Sabbath to the temporary legislation of the era of the law.[19]

CHAPTER 10

THE CHRISTIAN SABBATH VIEW

The Mosaic Law

In the fourth commandment of the Mosaic law, there is the statement "Remember the Sabbath day to keep it holy." The text further stipulates that no work was to be done on that day as part of the observance of the Sabbath.

Presentation of the Christian Sabbath View

The reason given for this commandment according to Exodus 20:11 is that God created the world in six days and rested on the seventh day. Then follows the statement, "Wherefore the Lord blessed the Sabbath day and hallowed it." This passage does seem to give a commentary on what God had done at creation. Having completed His work of creation in six days, He blessed and sanctified the Sabbath day <u>at creation</u>. Thus this evidences that the Sabbath day has stood from creation as a day set aside and sanctified by God, and then at Sinai it was incorporated into the ten commandments.

Thus the Sabbath is represented as a memorial of creation, and it was God's intention that it be observed by man from that hour. It would seem odd to be instituting a memorial of creation as late as Exodus.[1]

Objections to the Christian Sabbath View

It must be acknowledged that there are objections to this view. If the Sabbath was blessed and sanctified at creation, as this Christian Sabbath view maintains, how does one explain the fact that Sabbath observance seems to be a relatively new idea to the children of Israel? It is not until Exodus 16 that the first guidelines concerning Sabbath observance are given and it appears the people had a difficult time understanding the requirements at this point (see Exodus 16:25-31). Could not the command to "remember" the Sabbath of Exodus 20:8 refer to the statements and guidelines of Exodus rather than to something which happened at creation? And do not further passages of God's revelation, such as Ezekiel 20:12 and Nehemiah 9:14, say that the Sabbath was given to Israel at Sinai?

Answers to the Objections to the Christian Sabbath View

How does the Christian Sabbath view explain these objections? This position would argue that the matter can only be explained by a consideration of and proper understanding of the historical setting.

It is true, no doubt, that while Israel was in bondage in Egypt, she was not able to observe the Sabbath. Part of Moses' request to Pharaoh was that the children of Israel should be set free to go and sacrifice to the Lord and worship Him (Exodus 5:1-3). Then in Exodus 16, when guidelines for Sabbath observance were given, it was not an introduction of Sabbath observance, but a reminder and much needed instruction to help them understand what Sabbath observance is all about since it had not been observed for so long.

Further, mild treatment is prescribed for Sabbath-breakers in Exodus 16:25-30 because it is a learning experience for God's people as they move to a reinstatement of the Sabbath (Numbers 15:32-36).[2] The explanation of such passages as Ezekiel 20:12 and Nehemiah 9:14 is that the Sabbath in its specific Old Testament form does date from the time of Moses.[3] The explanation of the neglect of the Sabbath during the period of time before the giving of the law at Sinai is that it was a time when the demands of the law were not explicitly spelled out and some of the requirements were only dimly perceived.[4] That there must have been some knowledge of God's requirements before Mt. Sinai is clear in the story of Cain and Abel as murder is obviously forbidden.[5]

The Westminster Confession of Faith (WCF) identifies the law given to Adam with the commandments delivered by God to Moses (WCF 19:1-2). Thus Charles Hodge writes:

> As the observance of the Sabbath had died out among the nations, it was solemnly reenacted under the Mosaic dispensation to be a sign of the covenant between God and the children of Israel.[6]

But even this re-enactment of the law at Sinai was not its final form. As Beckwith states, the "Sabbath as a creation ordinance took a parenthetical form under the law."[7] And seeing the Sabbath as a memorial of creation[8] gives it a broader meaning and more solid foundation than to see it as existing just in the period of the law.

Even though the Sabbath did exist before the Mosaic law, it still had significance in the Mosaic law itself as a sign of the Mosaic covenant. It is represented as a memorial of redemption (Deuteronomy 5:12-15), which fact highlights the close connection between the Sabbath and Israel's redemption from Egypt. Worship and the Sabbath are given by God to a redeemed people as part of their "constitution" as a nation. Clearly it has an important place, not only as a creation ordinance, but also in the Mosaic law and the Mosaic covenant.

The Permanency of the Sabbath

The Christian Sabbath position does argue for the permanence of Sabbath observance from the following reasons.

1. The Sabbath is permanent because it is part of the Ten Commandments.

The very fact that the Sabbath became part of the Ten Commandments given by Moses is used as a strong argument for the permanency of the Sabbath. Surely, if any part of the Mosaic law is permanent, one would expect the Ten Commandments to be so.[9] The Sabbath commandment, it is contended, is a part of the <u>moral will of God</u>, with the moral will of God being defined as a law that "expresses an obligation arising out of our relations to God or out of our permanent relations to our fellow men."[10]

On the other hand, those commands of the Old Testament which were addressed to the "Jews as Jews and were founded on the peculiar circumstances and relations" of the nation of Israel are called <u>ceremonial</u>.[11] The moral law (the Ten Commandments) was written on stone and is therefore permanent.[12]

2. <u>The Sabbath is permanent because of the penalty attached to it.</u>

According to Exodus 31:14 the penalty of breaking the Sabbath commandment is death. No ceremonial law carried a capital offense.[13] Further, although a ceremonial law may be set aside, a moral law cannot be repealed because it is an expression of the very nature of God.[14]

Therefore, because of these facts the Sabbath commandment contains a moral imperative for the church today. It is moral in that there should be a day of rest, a cessation of our worldly activities and an entering into the worship of God.[15] If we are to worship God according to His revealed will and not according to our own devices, we need to set a day aside for that purpose. God gives us one day in seven to pursue Him.[16]

If this sounds legalistic and ritualistic, it is hard to see how only the Sabbath commandment can be labelled with these terms. Why not then also call the first, second, sixth and other commandments legalistic and ritualistic, if one asserts that these commands have a moral imperative for today?[17] Why are we alarmed at the breaking of some of the commandments, but not just as alarmed when the Sabbath command is flagrantly violated?[18]

As the Westminster Confession of Faith asserts in question 121 of the larger catechism, we need to remember the Sabbath because

. . . it cometh but once in seven days and many worldly businesses come between, and too often take off our minds from thinking of it, either to prepare for it, or to sanctify it; and that Satan with his instruments much labor to blot out the glory, and even the memory of it, to bring in all irreligion and impiety.

Whatever else may be said about the Sabbath commandment,[19] the prophets continued to call Israel back to its observance (Isaiah 58:13, Jeremiah 17:21-27 and Nehemiah 13:15-22), and they even made the faithful observance of the Sabbath one of the glories of the Messiah's reign.[20]

Conclusion

Therefore, according to the Christian Sabbath view, the Sabbath has stood from creation as God's requirement of man. It is a creation ordinance. Its permanence is evidenced in light of the fact that it is one of the Ten Commandments, part of the moral law, and it brought the penalty of death for failure to observe it.

Because of this it is a moral imperative for the church today. However, its observance is not mandated for the seventh day, as will be seen in future chapters.

CHAPTER 11

THE CHRISTIAN SABBATH VIEW

Jesus and the Sabbath

One of the key questions one faces concerning a continuation of Sabbath observance in our day has to do with the testimony of the New Testament. Does the New Testament sanction a continuing Sabbath observance? It is argued by some that there is no specific command in the New Testament that the believer is to observe the Sabbath. Neither is there, some would argue, any identification of the Lord's day with the Sabbath.[1] Therefore, what ground is there for a continuation for any Sabbath observance, especially an idea of a Christian Sabbath observance?

The lack of a clear pronouncement which makes the first day of the week the Christian Sabbath, it is replied, is not critical, since the Sabbath is part of the moral law, and once the moral law is given, it would take a direct declaration to repeal it. Therefore, since we have no such declaration, we must assume that the Sabbath commandment is still in force.[2]

But further than that, it is contended that Sabbath observance does not just come from the moral law, but is also tied to the greater fullness of redemption accomplished by Jesus Christ. If redemption from Egypt gave sanction to the Sabbath and provided reason for observing it (Deuteronomy 5:12-15), the greater redemption by Christ surely gives the Sabbath increased relevance, sanction and blessing.[3]

Jesus and the Sabbath

With these objections briefly answered, consideration is now given to the New Testament's overall witness to the Sabbath, beginning with the teaching and testimony of Christ Himself.

Jesus was strictly obedient to the Sabbath law during His earthly life.[4] He never gave any indication that the Sabbath would be completely abolished or set aside. Although it is true that a lot of His controversies with religious leaders were over the observance of the Sabbath, the problem was not the Sabbath itself but the Pharisaic interpretations of the Sabbath.[5] Clearly, Jesus seemed to treat the Sabbath differently than he treated ceremonial regulations. In fact, he dealt with the Sabbath as He did with the fifth, sixth and seventh commandments, showing that He regarded the Sabbath commandment in the same category as the other commandments.[6]

Further, Jesus' statement in Mark 2:27 that "the Sabbath was made for man and not man for the Sabbath" broadens the implications of the Sabbath beyond Judaism. This statement that the Sabbath was made for man (anthropos) suggests it was made for mankind as a whole.[7] That the Sabbath was made (ginomai) for man suggests a connection with the creation of the world.[8] It would also seem rather difficult for Jesus to declare lordship over something which would soon be eliminated and thus not a part of His kingdom.[9]

The Basis for a Change of Days

But what about the basis for a change from the seventh day to the first day of the week. The above arguments establish a basis for the continuation of the Sabbath. Is there any basis for arguing for a change of the day? The answer is that the lordship of Christ coupled with His work of redemption provides the basis for the change from the seventh day to the first day of the week. The fact that Christ as Lord was raised from the dead on the first day of the week, it is argued, is more than enough for the change. Also the redemption secured by Christ was full, final and complete.

Would not such a momentous event (Christ's redemption), which fulfilled much of the Old Testament, bring significant change? A central part of that redemption focused on the resurrection. Also the fact that Christ rose on the first day of the week set that day apart as a day of joy and gladness immediately.

Although the early Jewish Christians probably continued to worship on Saturday, as well as Sunday, a new pattern begins to emerge in the pages of the New Testament. That pattern is evidenced in Christ's example and the example of the apostles as they gave authority to make Sunday rather than Saturday the day of worship (John 20:1, 19, 26; Acts 20:7; 1 Corinthians 16:2; and Revelation 1:10).

Thus to continue to observe the seventh day as the Sabbath is in essence to assert that the redemptive event of the Exodus was more important that the redemptive work of Jesus Christ.[10] If the creation of the world required one sequence where rest falls at the end of the week then the epoch-making event of the recreation (as brought about by the resurrection) required another sequence where rest falls at the beginning of the week.[11] Such a change is also evidence of the present eschatological situation of the church where the new creation rest has been made available by Christ.[12]

Although these changes have taken place, the essence of the day remains basically the same. The day of Christ's resurrection comes to have all the spiritual and practical significance of the Old Testament Sabbath as a day of rest and worship.[13]

Conclusion

Clearly there is today a Christian Sabbath, according to the view we have been considering. Though there is no specific command concerning a continuation of Sabbath observance in the New Testament, such is not critical since the Sabbath is part of the moral law and the moral law has never been repealed.

Further evidence is found in the attitude and practice of the Lord Jesus Himself. He never gave any indication the Sabbath was or would be abolished. His controversies over the Sabbath were not over Sabbath observance itself, but over the Pharisaical interpretations of it. He did treat the Sabbath differently than the ceremonial regulations, so it seems true that for Him the Sabbath was part of the moral law. His statement concerning the Sabbath being made for man broadens the implications of the Sabbath beyond Judaism.

Finally, the basis for a change from the seventh to the first day of the week for the observance of the Sabbath is based on His Lordship and the fact that He was raised from the dead the first day of the week.

Thus there is clearly today a Christian Sabbath--a day of rest and worship on the first day of the week.

CHAPTER 12

THE CHRISTIAN SABBATH VIEW

The Lord's Day

The apostle John, writing about sixty years or more after the resurrection of Christ, uses the term "the Lord's Day" in Revelation 1:10. This expression is not to be equated with the Old Testament expression "the day of the Lord," nor is it a reference to Easter Sunday. Rather, it is the day upon which the early church proclaimed Jesus as Lord.[1] This day was the day belonging to the Lord.

This New Testament phrase, the Lord's Day, though not equal to any Old Testament word or phrase, does parallel an Old Testament concept used in Isaiah 58:13. In that passage the Sabbath is referred to as "my (the Lord's) holy day" and "the holy day of the Lord." Therefore both the Old Testament Sabbath and the Christian day of worship are called the Lord's day.[2]

Two Conclusions from the Fact
of a Lord's Day

Two conclusions can be drawn from this fact. First, not every day is the Lord's Day. It is true that every day can be consecrated to God by the believer, but not every day can be given over to rest, worship and service. The very phrase, "the Lord's Day," implies that one day, not every day, is special to the Lord.[3] The particular day which is observed is not a matter of indifference, but that day is a necessary consequence of the work and ministry of Christ.[4]

Second, the conclusion can be drawn that the Lord's Day is not essentially different from the Sabbath, but is a continuation of the Sabbath.[5] The Lord's Day and the Sabbath should be regarded as essentially one and the same institution.[6]

New Testament Believers Should Be Observing the Christian Sabbath

On these grounds the New Testament believer should be observing a Sabbath--not an Old Testament Sabbath, but the Christian Sabbath. It is the Lord's Day--the day the early church proclaimed Jesus as Lord. Not every day is the Lord's day, but it is a special day set apart for rest, worship and service. It is not essentially different from the Sabbath, but is a continuation of the Sabbath.

The modern neglect of the Sabbath, because of the claim that there is no clear New Testament command, shows the pitiful spiritual condition of the church today. Are God's people more interested in self-indulgence than in spiritual vitality? The church today is badly in need, it seems, of the spiritual stimulus which a day set apart for the Lord brings.[7]

Conclusion

The term "the Lord's Day" is a unique expression in the New Testament. Its use shows that one day and not every day is special to the Lord. This special day known as "the Lord's Day" is a continuation of the Sabbath and should be considered essentially one and the same institution. Thus it is clear that the New Testament believer should be observing a Sabbath.

But this New Testament Sabbath, the Christian Sabbath, is the Lord's Day spoken of above. It is the day the early church proclaimed Jesus as Lord.

The modern neglect of the Christian Sabbath evidences the weak spiritual condition of the church. It seems to indicate God's people today are more interested in their own pursuits and indulgence than in spiritual matters and proper worship of God.

CHAPTER 13

THE CHRISTIAN SABBATH VIEW

Sabbath Rest in Hebrews 3-4

It is important to understand that a day of rest is not commanded simply to free up a period of time for public and private worship. Such a reduction in meaning is a distortion of the Biblical perspective. It fails to appreciate the Sabbath rest as a future eternal hope.[1] In this vein Hebrews 3-4 becomes extremely important.

Two Themes in Hebrews

Two themes become prominent in the eschatological structure of the book of Hebrews: the themes of triumph and testing. The present time is characterized by both of these aspects--the triumph of Christ and the severe testing of the church.[2] By understanding the parallel between the church and Israel in 3:7-4:13, a proper conception of Sabbath rest follows. Although the Sabbath-Sunday issue cannot be solved solely on the basis of Hebrews 3-4, some significant matters of exegesis, which relate to the issue, can be clarified.[3]

Significant Matters of Exegesis

First, understand that Hebrews 3:7-4:13 rests on the assumption that believers under the new covenant are in a similar situation as Israel in the wilderness. Both are given the promise of rest (3:1 and 4:1). Both are exposed to similar trials and the danger of unbelief (3:12, 19 and 4:6). And both are exhorted to persevere in the faith (3:8, 14 and 4:1, 11). The church is a wilderness community or a pilgrim people who have a part in Christ's house if they hold fast to the end (3:6). The "if" leads to the exhortations which follow and leads to the development of the argument concerning Sabbath rest.[4]

It is important to see that the analogy between the church and Israel in the wilderness pictures God's people as on the way, waiting, but not yet having arrived at their destination.[5] This has ramifications for interpreting Hebrews 3-4. Follow carefully how the writer of Hebrews unfolds his argument.

He sandwiches Genesis 2:2 (Hebrews 4:4) between two quotations from Psalm 95:11 (Hebrews 4:3 and 5). Thus he is identifying the rest of Canaan (Psalm 95) with the Sabbath rest at creation (Genesis 2). Since the people did not enter that rest through Joshua, the rest still remains for the people of God to enter (Hebrews 4:8-9). However, because of the parallel situation between Israel in the wilderness and the church, this rest must be seen as entirely future. That is, Israel on their journey, even in Canaan though under the leadership of Joshua, did not enter into this rest. Therefore neither has the church in her journey entered into rest today.

Again, the point is stated that because of this parallelism between Israel in the wilderness and the church, this rest must be seen as entirely future. The issue is not whether the ultimate benefits of salvation are present. They are present as evidenced by the book of Hebrews (9:26 and 6:5) and Matthew 11:28. The issue is whether Hebrews 3:7-4:13 teaches that God's rest is present for the church. In reality the rest of Genesis 2 has been secured and guaranteed by Christ, but it is still entirely future and will not arrive until His return.[6]

The fact that God's rest is still entirely future is rooted in the wilderness setting of the church in Hebrews 3-4 and becomes decisive for understanding the remainder of the passage. The present tense of Hebrews 4:3 should be translated as "we will enter" (the present gives a future note of certainty here) or "we are entering" (a progressive entering is under way but not yet completed).[7]

The "today" picked up from Psalm 95 applies to the present situation of the readers or anytime the good news is proclaimed. In the context of Hebrews 3:4 there is reference to the wilderness time when faith in God's promise to enter rest is continually tempted to unbelief.[8] And the ceasing from "his works" in Hebrews 4:10 are not dead works but desert (wilderness) works; that is, they are not sinful works but the works of believers in the present wilderness situation. To interpret these works as "dead works" or "sinful works" presents a startling contradiction because Hebrews 4:10 draws a parallel between God's works and our works.[9]

Rest for the church, then is represented in Hebrews 3-4 as follows:

1. Entirely future
2. Sabbath-resting
3. Grounded in God's rest at creation.

Some Implications from the Argument in Hebrews 3-4

The church has not and does not enter into that rest during her wilderness journey. And although the author of Hebrews is not explicitly concerned about Sabbath-keeping under the new covenant, some implications can be drawn from the argument in Hebrews 3-4.[10]

First, the "rest" of Hebrews 4:9 implies a weekly Sabbath rest. The word for rest here is sabbatismos.[11] The word does not emphasize the Sabbath day itself, but the celebration rest connected with the Sabbath.[12] However, there does appear to be an inner connection between the future Sabbath rest and the ongoing Sabbath observance. A recurring Sabbath observance becomes a type of future rest. Genesis 2:2-3 is used elsewhere in Scripture, but only for instituting the weekly Sabbath. This is not completely outside the author's frame of reference. In fact, it is "a rather unlikely supposition" that the author of Hebrews used the term sabbatismos to speak of future rest, and then connected that rest with Genesis 2:2-3 without any thought of the weekly ordinance.[13] Thus the rest of Hebrews 4:9 implies a weekly Sabbath rest.

Second, the rest in Hebrews 3-4, because it is entirely future, implies that the weekly Sabbath still remains in force under the new covenant. To deny this is to suppose that the author of Hebrews believed " . . .the weekly sign has ceased even though the reality to which it points is still future." Surely this is another unlikely supposition.[14]

Third, the fact that the rest in Hebrews 3-4 is grounded in God's rest at creation supports the view that the weekly Sabbath is a creation ordinance. To deny this is to disagree with the author's own understanding of Genesis 2:2. He not only finds it to be a description of God's rest at creation, but he also sees it as the future mandate given by God that mankind enter and share that rest (Hebrews 3b-4, 6a).[15]

Conclusion

Hebrews 3:7-4:13 rests on the assumption that believers in the new covenant are in a similar situation as Israel in wilderness. Both are given the promise of rest. Both are exposed to trials and the danger of unbelief. Both are exhorted to persevere in faith. This rest of the church today is entirely future, coming at Christ's return.[16] The eschatological benefits of salvation are present today, but the rest is not. The rest of Hebrews 4:9 implies a weekly Sabbath rest. Also, the rest in Hebrews 3-4, because it is entirely future, implies the weekly Sabbath still remains in force under the new covenant. Further, the fact that the rest in Hebrews 3-4 is grounded in God's rest at creation supports the idea that the weekly Sabbath is a creation ordinance. Therefore, there is a Christian Sabbath.

CHAPTER 14

THE CHRISTIAN SABBATH VIEW

Paul and the Sabbath

Certainly Paul's view is an important part of the New Testament testimony concerning the Sabbath. His statements on the subject, however, in Colossians 2:16-17 contain some very derogatory remarks. In another text, Romans 14:5, he refers to freedom concerning the observance of days. How do these statements fit into the Christian Sabbath view that the Sabbath commandment is still binding on believers under the new covenant?

Colossians 2:16-17

These passages must be seen in light of their own context and the further context of Scripture. In Colossians 2:16-17 Paul is writing against false teaching composed of a combination of Jewish ritualism and an oriental, gnostic-type philosophy. A reference to "sabbaths" (plural) can only be a reference to the Jewish sabbaths and not to the first day of the week. Paul is denouncing any one who would judge on the basis of strictly Jewish practices.[1] It has, therefore, no reference to the Christian Sabbath.

Romans 14:5

In Romans 14:5, when Paul acknowledges each man can esteem one day above another and another man may esteem every day alike, he has specifically in mind the ceremonial holy days which some Jewish Christians were observing. If one interprets this passage to refer to the Christian Sabbath and contends that even this day can be set aside, this is obviously an erroneous interpretation. If no day has any special significance, including the Lord's day, then the apostle John in Revelation 1:10 is either misleading, or is in conflict with Paul, or John is cast in the role of the weaker brother.[2]

Conclusion

Therefore, it has been shown that neither Colossians 2:16-17 nor Romans 14:4 has in view the weekly Christian Sabbath.[3] The reason the Christian Sabbath is not emphasized in the New Testament is because the Jewish regulations had degenerated the Sabbath into legalistic ceremonialism. Christ and Paul do not abolish the law of the Sabbath, but rather they give it its true meaning.[4] The Sabbath commandment still stands under the new covenant because it is a creation ordinance and because the law still has a role in the life of a believer. The next chapter will discuss briefly that subject of the role of the law in the believer's life.

CHAPTER 15

THE CHRISTIAN SABBATH VIEW

The Role of the Law

The word "law" in the New Testament can have different meanings. Therefore, extreme care must be taken in evaluating the role of the law in the life of the believer.[1]

The Christian Is Free from the Law

Christians are free from the law in the sense that the law is not kept for salvation. The observance of the law must be taken out of the context of justification.[2] The liberty which Christ has purchased is freedom from the curse of the law and freedom from the yoke of the ceremonial law (WCF 20:1).

The Law Is a Benefit to the Believer

However, the law can have a very positive effect in the life of a believer, as evidenced in the following passages:

1. Romans 3:31--through faith we establish the law.

2. Romans 13:10--love is the fulfillment of the law.

3. 1 John 2:3--we know him if we keep his commandments.

4. 1 John 2:7--no new commandment . . . but an old commandment. . . . that you love one another.

5. 1 Corinthians 7:19--keeping the commandments of God is what matters.

Thus keeping the commandments of God is still very important to the believer. Since the Sabbath commandment is one of the Ten Commandments (the moral law), it would seem that keeping the Sabbath commandment would be important.

The Form of the Law
Different in Two Covenants

Yet it must be recognized that the form of the law in the new covenant is different from the form of the law in the Mosaic covenant. In the Old Testament the law was an external summation of the will of God written on stone tablets. The believer under the new covenant does not live under an externalized administration of the law, but he lives with the law written in his heart ministered by the Holy Spirit. Such a distinction "gives recognition to the fading form of law administration under the Mosaic covenant while also treating seriously the continued significance of the essence of that same law."[3]

Conclusion

Thus the central essence of the covenant of law does enter in an important way into the life of the New Testament believer. Full blessedness is a result of keeping God's law (Ephesians 6:1-3 and James 1:22). On the other hand, Christians who live unrighteously are chastened by the Lord (Hebrews 12:6). Christians will also be judged according to their works (2 Corinthians 5:10 and Revelation 20:12). These statements are not unrelated to the law. Since the Ten Commandments are a summary of God's will, they are still binding and have a role to play in the life of the believer.[4] It follows, therefore, that there would be a Christian Sabbath based on the fourth commandment.

CHAPTER 16

THE CHRISTIAN SABBATH VIEW

Sabbath and Sunday
in the Post-Apostolic Church

Several facts are clear concerning Sabbath and Sunday in the post-apostolic church.

First, the word Sabbath was used exclusively of the seventh day.[1]

Second, the first equation of Sunday with the Sabbath did not come until the fourth century.[2]

Third, the Jewish Sabbath almost disappears from recorded Christian practice after Christ's resurrection.[3] Early Jewish Christians probably observed both the Sabbath and Sunday until they were forced out of the synagogue, and then they concentrated on the Lord's Day as their weekly day of rest and worship.[4]

Also, the early church saw the Sabbath as a sign of the Mosaic covenant, which passed away with the coming of Christ. Thus the seventh day was no longer sacred to the Christian because it could not express all that the New Covenant meant.[5]

The Rise of a Theology of the Lord's Day

In place of the Sabbath a theology of the Lord's Day arose. As Ignatius expressed it at the end of the first century, "No longer observing sabbaths, but fashioning our lives according to the Lord's day."[6] The early church probably regarded the observance of Sunday in terms of a whole day set aside for the Lord. Sunday is compared with both the Jewish Sabbath and pagan festivals. In both cases these involved the whole day. Also believers are exhorted not to fast on Sunday, but to spend time in prayer avoiding anxious thoughts. This prohibition about fasting would involve the whole day as would the avoidance of anxious thoughts.[7]

Further, Origen makes a comment on Paul's words in Galatians concerning the observance of days.

> If anyone makes a rejoinder of this by talking of our observances of certain days, the Lord's Days, or the Preparation, or the Passover, or Pentecost, we would reply to this that the perfect man, who is always engaged in the words, works and thoughts of the Divine Logos, who is by nature his Lord, is always living in his days and is constantly observing the Lord's Days.[8]

Origen admits that in spite of Paul's words in Galatians, Christians do observe days with the Lord's Day being put first.[9]

Sunday Regarded
as a Holy Day and a Feast Day

The early church did view Sunday as a holy day. Dionysius, bishop of Corinth (168 A.D.), writes "Today we have passed the Lord's holy day. . . " The Didascalia (230 A.D.) states, "For not even on Sundays, in which we rejoice and make good cheer, is it permitted to anyone to speak a word of levity or one of alien religion."[10]

The early church also viewed Sunday as a feast day where worship, rejoicing and the remembering of the spiritual blessings in Christ took place.[11]

Sunday Also Regarded
as a Day of Rest

Since Sunday was seen as a holy day and a feast day, it followed that Sunday would also be seen as a day of rest. Some have thought that the statements of the early church fathers against laziness would mean that ordinary work would have continued Sunday.[12] However, even on the days of the pagan festivals, ordinary work was put aside. So when Tertullian makes the comparison between the

Christian sacred days and those of the Jews and pagans, it seems certain that he implies that all ordinary work is to be put aside.[13] Evidence for this view is found in Clement of Alexandria, Tertullian in North Africa, Hippolytus in Rome, Origen in Alexandria and the <u>Didascalia</u> in Syria.[14]

Sunday Is Substituted for the Sabbath

Eusebius of Caeserea is an important person because he is a bridge between the church before and after Constantine. In his comments on Psalm 92 (<u>Commentary on the Psalms</u>, written about eight years after Constantine's decree of 321 A.D.) he draws a connection between the Jewish Sabbath and the Christian Sunday. Both were opportunities meant for the knowledge of God. Sunday is now substituted for the Sabbath for "on that day [Sunday] we ourselves coming together at intervals of six days are celebrating holy and spiritual sabbaths."[15]

The question is clear. Is this connection which Eusebius makes between the Sabbath and Sunday an entirely new connection, or is it influenced by Constantine's decree in 321 A.D. which says that no work was to be done on Sunday? Eusebius stresses that what he has been saying about Christian worship was handed down to him. This was a tradition of the church. And, much of the conceptions Eusebius uses can be found in earlier church fathers.

What is new is the way Eusebius puts them together into a consistent whole.[16] There is no indication Eusebius has Constantine's decree in mind. The decree was purely negative. Its intention was to empty the day of ordinary work. Instead of Constantine originating the attitude of Sunday in its relation to the Sabbath, he was more likely following earlier practices.[17]

Conclusion

Therefore the conclusion of this chapter must be that rather early in the history of the church a theology of the Lord's Day arose. It included the concept of a whole day to be set aside for the Lord. It was a holy day set aside for worship and remembrance of Christ and His blessings and also for rest. It was the Christian Sabbath.

CHAPTER 17

THE CHRISTIAN SABBATH VIEW

Practical Application

It should be no surprise that those who basically agree on the continuing moral imperative of the Sabbath commandment do not always agree on some of the particulars. It is generally agreed by those of this view that the Sabbath commandment includes rest from labor, the worship of God, and works of necessity. But what about such activities as watching television, reading the newspaper, participating in sports or other activities?[1]

Two Negative Paths to Avoid

At this point the opponents of Sabbath observance "peddle the charge of pharisaism." The main question, however, is whether the Sabbath is a divine ordinance or not. If it is, then adherence to it is not legalistic. The charge of pharisaism could be evidence that our consciences have become insensitive to the holiness of the demands of the Sabbath law.[2]

However, there is the danger that one might "encumber the institution of God with . . . our own inventions." To add to the requirements of God does usurp His authority, which is the essence of impiety and lawlessness. Also, we must avoid the danger of making Sabbath observance an instrument of self-righteousness.[3]

Thus two negative paths must be avoided--the one of legalism and the other of lawlessness.

A Positive Path to Be Pursued

The Sabbath commandment is part of that perfect law of liberty. It is best observed by following Biblical principles within the context of individual circumstances, where a person is fully persuaded in his own mind but does not judge others.[4]

The New Testament does not give to the church a list of do's and don't's in relation to the Lord's Day, but there are Scriptural principles that should help in observance of Sunday as the Lord's Day.[5] These principles fall into two categories.

First, the Lord's Day should be a day of rest. The word "Sabbath" means to cease. Thus we should stop doing those things on the Lord's Day which take up so much of our time during the week in employment and recreation.[6]

Second, there should be a priority on corporate worship with God's people. We rest from our normal labor so we can worship God properly. Personal time should also be set aside for the study of God's word and prayer.[7]

Third, there should be an emphasis on fellowship and doing good. Christ's own example showed that certain kinds of works are appropriate and legitimate. These include works of piety (work done, for example, by pastors so God can be worshipped), works of necessity (works that cannot be delayed without harm to life or property), and works of mercy.[8] Christ also accepted meal invitations, so the necessary work required for preparing meals received His endorsement.[9]

The Place of the Government

In any discussion of the practical observance of the Lord's Day, the question usually arises as to what role the government should play in enforcing Sunday observance. In other words, what about blue laws? There does not seem to be agreement on this matter by the proponents of the Christian Sabbath view. On the one hand, some want to stress the importance of an external regulation to ensure respect for the Lord's Day. Although there are drawbacks to a mere external imposition of conduct, there are also benefits to society.[10]

For example, the observance of a Sabbath produces a restraining influence upon unbelievers, promotes public order, and helps preserve our most cherished rights and liberties.[11]

On the other hand, not all who hold strongly to the idea and practice of a Christian Sabbath observance would want to return to the blue laws.[12] Instead, they would favor effort being put into positive teaching concerning the benefits that would result from a day of worship and rest. Also there should be protection for those who are compelled to work on the Sabbath.[13] A person should have the option not to work on his or her particular Sabbath. As society moves more and more toward secularization, the challenge is not just the right kind of legislation, but the right kind of principles set forth in the homes, schools and churches with confidence that God's power can change lives.[14]

Perhaps the most important question related to the Lord's Day is not "What may I do or not do on the Sabbath?" but "How may I make the most of this day for Christ.?"[15]

Conclusion

Those who hold to the Christian Sabbath view are not agreed in all matters pertaining to its practical application. All are agreed that there should be respect for and observance of the first day of the week. All are agreed it is to be a day of worship and rest. Beyond these principles there seems to be a tension as to how to balance proper Sabbath observance without veering off into the advocacy of our own inventions and thus make it an instrument of self-righteousness. All of this view would agree that the two extremes are legalism and lawlessness, but the middle point of balance is not always clear to all.

Noting that the New Testament does not give a list of do's and don't's, there would be agreement on several matters. First, this day should be a day of rest from our normal daily routine of life. Second, there should be a priority on worship with the people of God. Third, there should be an emphasis on fellowship and doing good.

The place of the government in relation to enforcement is also a point of disagreement. Some favor a government recognition of the one day because of its benefit to man and society, but not all desire the establishment of blue laws.

All of the above does make the application of the Christian Sabbath a difficult matter, but advocates would not see it to be impossible as it is taught in Scripture.

PART THREE

THE LORD'S DAY VIEW

CHAPTER 18

THE LORD'S DAY VIEW

God's Rest at Creation

Two views of the Sabbath have been presented thus far. One says there is a direct relation between the Sabbath and the New Testament believer today--the Seventh Day view. The second says there is an indirect relation between the Old Testament Sabbath and the church today--the Christian Sabbath view. Now for several chapters another position will be analyzed--the Lord's Day view. This position says there is no relationship between the Old Testament Sabbath and our worship practices today.

Two recent books have set forth this conviction. Willy Rordorf has written Sunday, while D.A. Carson has edited a work titled From Sabbath to Lord's Day. Although these two books are very different in their handling of the material and also in some of their major conclusions, they are, on the other hand, in agreement in the view that Sunday worship has no relationship to the fourth commandment of the Mosaic law.[1]

Part of the issue is how the concept of physical rest relates to and applies to our worship practices today. Willy Rordorf maintains that it is difficult to justify Sunday rest by any other means than by referring to the sabbath commandment, yet this approach, he feels, brings too many theological problems.[2] The book edited by D.A. Carson argues against any kind of a Sabbath "transfer theology" where Sunday becomes the Christian Sabbath. According to Carson, Sunday is not a substitute for the Sabbath and has no relationship to the fourth commandment.[3]

The following chapters will set forth this position beginning with the consideration of God's rest at creation.

God's Creation Rest Did Not Establish
a Creation Ordinance

In presenting the first two views, the Seventh Day and the Christian Sabbath view, the discussion of the subject has begun with God's rest at creation, considering especially Genesis 2:2-3. A key question has been whether God's rest at creation was or was not part of a creation ordinance which is to be sustained in ages to come.

It is the conviction of the Lord's Day view that though Genesis 2:2-3 does conclude the creation account by showing that God rested on the seventh day, and though He blessed and sanctified the seventh day, all this has no relation to the Sabbath, for no mention is made here of the Sabbath. Nothing is said about a religious feast day or institution. Neither is there a direct command that the seventh day is to be kept.[4] The description of the seventh day centers solely on God and not on humanity.

God's Sanctifying of the Sabbath at Creation
Is Related to the Created World

The Lord's Day view does acknowledge that the blessing and sanctifying of the seventh day in Genesis does have some relation to the created world. Admittedly, the nature of that relation is extremely important. To understand this importance and its meaning, it must be seen that the seventh day is different from the other six days of creation in Genesis. The seventh day does not have a morning and evening, while the other six days do.[5] Thus it is not the seventh day as a seventh day that is blessed and sanctified here, but it is the goal of creation, that is, God's rest, which is blessed and sanctified. But how God's rest works itself out in the world awaits further unfolding,[6] which is to say the significance of the Sabbath is really future.

Conclusion

Thus there is no hint of a creation ordinance in Genesis 2.[7] God's rest on the seventh day becomes an eschatological sign pointing to a future rest.[8] The focus is not on continuing some creation ordinance, but on the divine ordering of history so that as history moves toward its consummation, it also moves toward the goal of God's rest. Thus according to the Lord's Day position, Genesis 1-2 does not impose a creation ordinance which man must observe and maintain through history, but it imposes a Sabbatical structure on the history of creation and the world.[9]

CHAPTER 19

THE LORD'S DAY VIEW

The Mosaic Law

The Sabbath Not Given Till Mt. Sinai

It has been pointed out that the Lord's Day view does not see God's creation rest as part of a creation ordinance. But this position does see the concept of God's rest working itself out in history in the Sabbath commandment given to Israel. This fourth commandment was one means of trying to restore the rest that sin had destroyed.[1] However, the Sabbath institution, where one day in seven was set aside for rest and worship, was not given by God until the giving of the law on Mt. Sinai. The Sabbath was not listed in God's covenant with Noah nor was it mentioned in Acts 15 where Gentiles were asked to observe certain Jewish regulations to help further fellowship with Jewish believers (the regulations in Acts 15 are based on the Noahic command[2]).

Implications of the Sabbath Originating at Mt. Sinai

Exodus 16 is the first real mention of the keeping of the Sabbath and it seems the people were not familiar with its observance (Exodus 16:27-31).[3] The fact that the Sabbath became the sign of the Mosaic covenant underlines the fact that it was given to Israel only and that it lasts only for the duration of the Mosaic covenant and that it derives its significance from the Mosaic covenant.[4]

The fact that the Sabbath originated at Mt. Sinai, as we have seen as the Lord's Day view, also means that the seven-day week originated at Mt. Sinai. Although there were periods of seven days duration in the ancient Near East long before the history of Israel, they were not calculated like the week we know today. The seven day periods in the ancient Near East reflect a simple observable calculation based on the phases of the moon.[5]

Exodus 20:11 Does Not Establish the Sabbath as a Creation Ordinance

Exodus 20:11 has been used many times to argue that at creation God blessed the Sabbath. Exodus 20:8-11 reads:

> Remember the Sabbath day to keep it holy. Six days you shall labor and do all your work, but the seventh day is the Sabbath of the Lord your God. In it you shall not do any work . . . For in six days the Lord made the heavens and the earth . . . and rested the seventh day. Wherefore the Lord blessed the Sabbath day and hallowed it.

Though other views see the last sentence above as referring back to the time of creation, the Lord's Day view differs. Rather than referring back to creation, it is an explanation of God's blessing activity in connection with the new institution of the Sabbath. There is a parallel not an equality between God's blessing activity of the seventh day and His blessing activity of the Sabbath.[6]

The above explanation of Exodus 20:11 is based on two considerations. First, in Deuteronomy 5:15 the Sabbath commandment is based on a previous historical event. The passage says God rescued Israel out of Egypt through a mighty hand and outstretched arm. The text continues, "Therefore the Lord thy God commanded thee to keep the sabbath day." Thus the keeping of the Sabbath is based upon God's deliverance from Egypt. Exodus 20:11 should be read the same way. God rested at creation, therefore He blessed the Sabbath now--at Mt. Sinai. Thus it is not a reference to the hour of creation, but to the hour of the giving of the law.

Second, the Hebrew particle translated "therefore" occurs in both Exodus 20:11 and Deuteronomy 5:15. It is used in the Pentateuch to connect an event in the past with a situation sometime later. It can be translated "consequently now." Thus again the Sabbath was not blessed at creation but rather at the giving of the law on Mt. Sinai.[7]

Purposes of the Sabbath

Again, according to the Lord's Day view, the Sabbath had several purposes. It served as a sign of the Mosaic covenant (Exodus 31:12-17). Now that the covenant was established between God and Israel, the Sabbath was given to help set the people apart for God. It thus became a sign of sanctification. Again it served to remind the people of God's great acts, being a memorial of creation (Exodus 20:11 and 31:17) and a memorial of redemption (Deuteronomy 5:15).[8]

The most characteristic feature of the Sabbath commandment at Sinai was its prohibition of work. It was a day of physical rest. Not even in the busiest times of plowing and harvest was there to be work on the Sabbath (Exodus 34:21). Physical rest, in turn, allowed for the activity of worship (Leviticus 23:2), but worship was not a major focus of the Sabbath institution in the Old Testament. In Deuteronomy 5:15, where all the servants and animals are to rest on the Sabbath, a strong humanitarian concern is stressed, and not worship. By stopping all work the Israelites demonstrated their obedience and complete consecration to God.[9]

The Sabbath in Later Old Testament History

Later in Old Testament history after the Exile there was a renewed emphasis on the Sabbath and the strictness of its observance. The Sabbath, along with circumcision and the study of the Torah, became a distinguishing mark of the nation of Israel. And although the emphasis in the early parts of the Old Testament was on physical rest and not so much on worship, the Exile changed things. A renewed emphasis upon worship after the Exile can be seen in Ezekiel 46 and Psalm 92.

Yet the most striking development concerning the Sabbath occurred during the period between the two testaments where the detailed legislation of the Jewish law, known as the Halakah, arose. How the Sabbath was to be observed was set forth, along with fine distinctions concerning what constituted work.[10] These detailed regulations provide a background for understanding Jesus' approach to the Sabbath question.

Conclusion and Summary

To summarize the Lord's Day view of the Sabbath in the Mosaic law, the following must be noted. First, negatively, the Sabbath in the Mosaic covenant was not based on any creation ordinance given in Genesis. Neither is it based on the Noahic covenant. Rather the Sabbath originated at Mt. Sinai and is based on the previous historical event of Israel's deliverance from Egypt. It was a sign of the Mosaic covenant and also a sign of Israel's sanctification. It was given to Israel only and lasts only the duration of the Mosaic covenant.

CHAPTER 20

THE LORD'S DAY VIEW

Jesus and the Sabbath

Jesus' attitude toward the Sabbath and the controversies in His ministry about the Sabbath provide the initial foundation and framework concerning the New Testament's testimony on the subject. In fact, the way Jesus handles the Sabbath is also an indicator of the way He handles the law.[1]

The setting and background for Jesus' controversies concerning Sabbath observance is the accumulated detailed regulations concerning the Sabbath found in the Halakah. It was difficult to distinguish between the added regulations in the Halakah and the Sabbath command itself. Even the major writers today on the Lord's Day view, Carson and Rordorf, evidence a difference of opinion, as we shall see, on this matter.

Luke 4:16

Luke 4:16 notes that Jesus went into the synagogue on the Sabbath as was His custom. The question arises as to how significant this custom of Jesus actually was. The use of this phrase "as was his custom" is only used elsewhere by Luke in Acts 17:2 where Paul's ministry is in view. It speaks here also of Paul's custom to attend the synagogue. Paul used the synagogue as an opportunity to teach and evangelize. Jesus also, according to the Lord's Day view, used the synagogue for teaching opportunities it presented Him. Such action does not reflect a theological commitment to the Sabbath.[2]

Thus the conclusion is that Luke 4:16 cannot be used to build any case that Jesus had a commitment to the Sabbath as a necessary time of worship. It merely afforded Him an opportunity to teach and preach.

Sabbath Controversies

It does not appear that Jesus goes out of His way to stir up controversy concerning the Sabbath, but his actions in the fulfillment of His ministry do cause controversy to arise. Once controversy begins to surface, Sabbath legislation based on the Halakah is used against Jesus.[3] Several of those controversies will now be considered in more detail.

Controversy One: Matthew 12:1-8, Mark 2:23-28 and Luke 6:1-5

Two samples of Sabbath controversy occur back to back in the Synoptic gospels. The first is in Matthew 12:1-8, Mark 2:23-28 and Luke 6:1-5. In this first controversy the disciples pluck some heads of grain (Luke adds "rubbing them in their hands") as they pass through a grain field on the Sabbath. The Pharisees point out that this is unlawful. Jesus responds with the Old Testament example of David and his company eating the showbread, which is only lawful for the priests to eat.

Carson notes that Jesus' appeal to David's example shows that in principle the Sabbath law might be set aside by other considerations.[4] Max Turner points out that these two leaders of Israel (David and Jesus) at least occasionally (and Jesus perhaps permanently) have the authority to transcend the law and its institutions.[5]

Matthew adds the example of the priests who profane the Sabbath in doing their work are blameless. Just as the Old Testament made provisions for a certain group of people with authority to override the Sabbath, so Jesus Himself has authority to override the Sabbath because of His work.[6]

Then each of these three gospels follows the controversy about plucking the grain with an explanatory statement concerning Jesus' Lordship over the Sabbath. He claims the authority to supercede the Sabbath without guilt.[7]

Mark precedes Jesus' statement about lordship over the Sabbath with the statement, "The Sabbath was made for man and not man for the Sabbath" (2:27). This statement, according to the Lord's Day view, should not be seen as a support for the creation ordinance view. The verb "was made" (ginomai) should not be understood as "created," but as "became" according to its use in Mark 4:37. Thus this verse is to be interpreted as stating that the Sabbath arose or came into existence for man at Mt. Sinai.[8] The use of the word "man" (anthropos) is not necessarily a reference to all mankind.[9]

Luke probably omitted the statement in Mark 2:27 for two reasons. First, it is omitted to strengthen the Christological comparison between David and Jesus. Second, it is omitted to eliminate a relatively obscure step in the logic of Jesus' teaching.[10] The fact that Jesus is Lord of the Sabbath raises the possibility of a future change or reinterpretation of the Sabbath. Thus the concept of Sabbath begins to undergo a transformation.[11]

Controversy Two: Matthew 12:9-14, Mark 3:1-6 and Luke 6:6-11

The second example of controversy brings into sharper focus the reasons for the controversy. The Scribes and Pharisees are watching Jesus closely to see if He will heal on the Sabbath, which He did. If so, they will bring an accusation against Him. Although the law says nothing about healing on the Sabbath, the rabbis interpreted healing as work, which was not to be done on the Sabbath.[12] Jesus used this opportunity to show that it was appropriate to do good on the Sabbath. Thus He healed the man.

This healing incident brings out an important distinction. Rordorf argues that Jesus attacks the Sabbath commandment itself, not just the Pharisees' interpretation of the Sabbath command.[13] He contends that if one of the Old Testament commandments got in Jesus' way as He carried out His work, He exercised sovereign power and pushed it aside. The Sabbath commandment was thus annulled by Jesus healing on the Sabbath.[14]

The authors in the Carson book take a different approach. It is not the Sabbath commandment itself that Jesus is breaking, but the Halakah, that is the interpretation of the Sabbath commandment. It is the strict legalism of the Pharisees that has to be attacked.[15] The fact that Jesus is not attacking the Sabbath commandment here should not be pressed too far. That is, it should not be pressed to the extent as to provide a positive hallowing of the Sabbath so that it now becomes a particularly appropriate day for healing. The force of the argument is that Jesus will not allow the Halakah to interfere with His redemptive mission.[16] There is certainly no hint in Jesus' ministry that the first day of the week should take on the character of Sabbath and replace it.[17]

Jesus Attitude toward the Law

Jesus' attitude toward the Sabbath must be assessed in light of His relation toward the law itself. But what then was Jesus' attitude toward the law? Part of the difficulty of this question is that although Jesus was a messenger of the new covenant, He lived under the old covenant. His teaching anticipates change, but that change does not come until after the resurrection.[18]

Matthew 5:17-20 is a passage where Jesus talks about the law. However, it should not be seen as a cure-all passage for the Sabbath. The passage in part states:

17) Think not that I am come to destroy the law, or the prophets; I am not come to destroy, but to fulfill.
18) For verily I say unto you, till heaven and earth pass, one jot or one tittle shall in no wise pass from the law, till all be fulfilled.

If "abolish" (destroy in the text above) in 5:17 is taken in the absolute sense, then Jesus made a mistake concerning food laws in Mark 7:19 where He declared all food clean. If "fulfillment" means "to show the true meaning of," then Christ came to show the true meaning of the Sabbath law. A survey of the New Testament must be made to see how this view applies to the Sabbath theme.[19]

One mistake to avoid in Matthew 5:17-20 and the rest of the gospels, according to Carson, is to read into the law some kind of moral, ceremonial, and civil distinction. This is not to deny that the moral law (in the sense of unchangeable prescriptions of right and wrong) exists. Neither is it to deny that some laws are ceremonial and others civil. The question is whether the New Testament writers use this distinction in establishing a relationship between law and gospel or in establishing what continues as authoritative in the New Testament from the Old Testament.[20]

However, even if such distinctions did apply, the Sabbath law, says Carson, seems to fall into the category of ceremonial law. Both David's law-breaking concerning the showbread and the priests' law-breaking in Matthew 12:1-8 come from the ceremonial law. This would seem to put the Sabbath in the ceremonial category with them.[21] Rordorf also puts the Sabbath in the ceremonial category where he comments that Jesus was opposed to any external observance of the ceremonial law, as seen in His attitude toward the Sabbath.[22] Obviously, if the Sabbath is placed in the ceremonial category, it no longer has binding force upon the believer.

Although Jesus in His teaching does not violate the law itself, He does modify, intensify and invest the Old Testament law with deeper meaning.[23] And with Jesus' ministry and the coming of the kingdom of God, the issue of the people's relation to the law becomes more complex. In fact, the law loses its central and mediating position and is replaced by the person and teaching of Jesus Himself.[24] Jesus does validate the law, but He also transcends the law in His own demands. The demands of the law remain in force only within His teaching (where they are modified by His own claims). The law, therefore, no longer has any merit on its own.[25] Jesus never treats the decalogue as a perfect sum of moral teaching.[26] Instead, that which is moral is now to be judged in reference to His own teaching and ministry.[27] In some cases there will be affirmation and continuance to the law and in other cases there will be discontinuance.[28]

The Sabbath commandment falls into the area of discontinuity, that is, it is not to be continued. The controversies surrounding the Sabbath in Matthew 12 follow Jesus' statement about coming to Him for true rest. The passages in Mark 2:23-3:6 and Luke 6:1-11 follow Jesus' comments about putting new wine in new wineskins, a statement which shows that there needs to be a complete renewal of religious terms. The application to the Sabbath is then brought out in Jesus' controversy with the Pharisees.[29]

Rordorf agrees with this view. He notes that Christ brought true rest and thus caused the hard-and-fast commandment to rest every seventh day to lose its importance.[30] He is convinced further that Sabbath theology parallels temple theology. As worshipping in one place passes away with the temple, so worshipping on one day passes away with the Sabbath. Instead of being confined to one day, the Sabbath came to mean the entire present age.[31]

To summarize the Lord's Day position concerning Jesus, the law and the Sabbath, note the following. First, the Sabbath law falls into the category of ceremonial law. On this basis, obviously, the Sabbath requirement is no longer binding on the believer. Second, Jesus' authority is now supreme. He establishes the law, but He also transcends the law. All morality must be weighed in light of His teaching and ministry. Such weighing will at times bring affirmation (agreement) with the law, but at other times it will bring discontinuity (disagreement) with the law. The Sabbath falls into this area of discontinuity. The bottom line is a removal of the believer from any obligation to keep a Sabbath commandment.

John 5:16-18

John 5:16-18 is another important passage dealing with the Sabbath. Again controversy has arisen over Jesus' healing on the Sabbath. In response He answers, "My Father has been working until now and I have been working." Thus the charge that Jesus works on the Sabbath is answered with the saying that He is only imitating His Father. The "until now," according to the Lord's Day view, signifies the end of an activity. The time will come when God and Jesus will cease from their work of salvation. The point of cessation is Jesus' death and resurrection which will inaugurate God's rest. Thus what is signified in the Sabbath is fulfilled in Christ. Christ's resurrection will fulfill the rest signified by the Old Testament Sabbath. The cessation from labor in the Sabbath commandment yields to the ceaseless activity of Jesus in accomplishing salvation which will yield the perfect Sabbath age. Thus the concept of literal, physical rest has been transformed by Christ's work of salvation.[32]

Rordorf draws out the implications concerning Jesus' attitude and view of the Sabbath when he notes that Sunday and the Jewish Sabbath have different roots. Sunday should not be thought of as inheriting and continuing the traditions of the Old Testament Sabbath.[33]

Conclusion

There exists no evidence that Jesus possessed a commitment to the Sabbath as the necessary day of worship. It was His custom to go to the synagogue on the seventh day, but this action must be seen as His simply taking advantage of a crowd to teach and minister. Jesus even indicated that the Sabbath law could be set aside in light of other considerations when he referred to David eating the showbread on the Sabbath. This also indicates that He has power to transcend the law and its institutions, including the Sabbath.

Even the statement that the Sabbath was made for man and not man for the Sabbath is to be interpreted to say that the Sabbath arose and came into existence for man at Mt. Sinai and not at creation. Thus it is not a creation ordinance, and it is part of the Mosaic law, and therefore Christ can and does set it aside.

Again, the Sabbath is seen as being part of the ceremonial law and not the moral law. Clearly if this is so, it is no longer binding upon the New Testament believer.

One must also in this discussion consider Jesus' attitude toward the law. His view is that the law is no longer in its central and mediating position, but has been replaced by His authority and teaching. He transcends the law. The demands of the law remain in force only within His teachings. The law only has merit now, therefore, if and when it has been affirmed by Him. In some cases of the law He will affirm it and in others He will disaffirm it, as He did the Sabbath.

CHAPTER 21

THE LORD'S DAY VIEW

The Origin of Sunday Worship

If there exists no relation of transference between the Sabbath commandment and Sunday worship, the question rises concerning the origin of Sunday worship. The Lord's Day view acknowledges that Christ's resurrection fulfills the Sabbath rest, and the fact that the resurrection takes place on the first day of the week and not on the seventh day provides a link between the days (even though the link says nothing about a Christian day of rest.).[1]

The Early Church Observed the Sabbath

This link between the two days was not made absolutely clear until later. Early Jewish believers in Christ continued to worship on the Sabbath in the temple and synagogues. No Jewish Christians were persecuted or even challenged about their Sabbath observance in the book of Acts or in the Epistles. Even in the Jewish/Gentile conflicts the Sabbath is never mentioned. With the exception of Stephen, the early church in Acts made its claims for Jesus without drawing the line back to the law. There is no firm evidence that the teaching of Jesus had any significant effect on the pattern of Jewish/Christian Sabbath observance. The Sabbath then followed as a matter of course.[2] The early church did observe the Sabbath.

Evidence for the Origin of Sunday Worship Is Scarce

Any evidence for the origin of Sunday worship is very scarce.[3] One possibility is that Sunday worship originated in the period of the resurrection appearances, since these appearances all took place on Sunday (see especially John's

Gospel). Perhaps John meant to draw a parallel between the apostles weekly meetings with the risen Lord on Sunday and the later weekly meetings of the church, but this can only be a guess. Thus the accounts of the resurrection narratives provide no demonstrable case that Sunday worship originated at that time.[4]

Another possibility is that Sunday worship originated in the Palestinian Jewish/Christian churches. Although there is no early direct evidence, by the second century Sunday worship appears as a universal practice outside Palestine. The likely explanation is that Sunday worship was already a Christian custom before the Gentile mission of the early church.[5]

The early Christians inherited from the Old Testament the weekly cycle. Although they eventually freed themselves from the Sabbath, they kept the Jewish week and the Jewish system of enumeration. The phrase "the first day of the week" was the Jewish reckoning for Sunday.[6] It is significant that a Gentile writer, Luke, in Acts 20, when he refers to the first day of the week, refers to the observance of a Jewish weekly cycle by a Gentile church. This must be taken as deliberate and may serve as an echo of the resurrection tradition.[7] In John 20:19 it was on the evening of the first day of the week that Jesus appeared to the disciples. The reference is to Sunday evening, which Acts 20 must also have in mind.[8]

The connection in Acts 20 between the "first day of the week," "to gather together," and "to break bread" are similar to later statements used to refer to Sunday worship (see 1 Corinthians 11:20, Didache 14:1 and Ignatius' Epistle to the Ephesians 20:2).[9] 1 Corinthians 16:2 also mentions the first day of the week. Paul says money is to be set aside on that day. Although Acts 20:7 and 1 Corinthians 16:2 are not completely unambiguous evidence for Sunday observance, yet seen in the light of later evidence there is strong presumption that these passages are good evidence for early Sunday observance.[10]

Why Sunday Was Chosen

Why was Sunday chosen? The Christians needed a time for distinctly Christian worship. When they went to look for an appropriate day, Sunday would immediately come to mind as a commemoration of the resurrection. However there is no hint of any Sabbatical associations. Sunday was not a substitute for the Sabbath nor was it related to the Sabbath commandment. Simply by the authoritative custom of the apostolic church, Sunday became the day on which Christians worship.[11]

Summary and Conclusion

Thus in answer to the question concerning the origin of Sunday as a day of worship for the early church, several ideas have been noted.

Evidence for the origin of Sunday worship is scarce. One can only speak of possibilities. Perhaps Sunday worship originated in the period of the resurrection appearances, which took place on Sunday. Perhaps Sunday worship originated in the Palestinian Jewish/Christian churches.

Whatever the case, it seems somewhere in early church history, when the Christian needed a time for distinctly Christian worship, Sunday appropriately came to mind as a commemoration of the resurrection.

Again, whatever the case and whenever it happened, there was no relation between the establishment of Sunday as the day of worship and the Sabbath commandment. It came only by authoritative apostolic custom.

CHAPTER 22

THE LORD'S DAY VIEW

The Lord's Day

Although the phrase "the Lord's Day" is used only once in the New Testament (Revelation 1:10), it is basic to a consideration of the origin and significance of the Christian weekly day of worship and is thus the subject of much debate.[1] Both Rordorf and the authors of the Carson book believe that this phrase does not refer to the eschatological day of the Lord or even to Easter, but rather they believe it refers to Sunday.[2]

The one use of the phrase "the Lord's Day" is in Revelation 1:10. The central theme of this book of Revelation is the concept of sovereignty. It tells of a tremendous battle which is being fought between the powers of Satan and the followers of Christ. His right to victory and sovereignty came because of His death and resurrection. He Who rules the world is the Lord and not the Emperor.[3] Christians will also be victorious because they worship the Lord.

Given this background it is easy to see how the day of Christ's resurrection from the dead, which was also the day Christians worshipped, would be called the Lord's day. The worship of the church marks out Christ's sphere of Lordship in the present world.[4] Thus the emphasis on the first day of the week in the resurrection narratives of John's Gospel, Acts 20:7 and 1 Corinthians 16:2 serve as a forerunner of the Lord's day.[5]

It is important to understand, however, that the Lord's Day was not observed as a literal day of rest, nor was observance of it associated with the Sabbath commandment.[6] For a long time Sunday was a day of work and the early church had to meet in the evenings for their worship as reflected in Acts 20:7.[7]

Summary

Thus according to the Lord's Day view the phrase "Lord's Day" is important in the present discussion. It refers to Sunday. It is called the Lord's day in the one Biblical reference of Revelation 1:10. Because of the theme of the book of Revelation (the battle between Satan and the followers of Christ), it is easy to see how the day of Christ's resurrection, which was also the day Christians worshipped, would be called the Lord's Day. But it was not observed as a literal day of rest, nor was it related to the Sabbath commandment of the Mosaic law.

CHAPTER 23

THE LORD'S DAY VIEW

Paul and the Sabbath

Paul's comments concerning the Sabbath are best understood in light of his view of the law. From the time of his conversion on the Damascus Road, Paul began to realize that God was now active in Jesus Christ rather than in the law of the Mosaic covenant.[1] This concept is clearly reflected in Paul's letters and has a relation to his view of the Sabbath.

Galatians 3:6

In Galatians 3:6 Paul begins to deal with the covenant made with Abraham and its relation to the Mosaic covenant. Clearly, in the area of justification and sonship, according to Paul, the law has no place. With the coming of Christ and the acceptance of the Gentiles on the basis of faith (in line with the Abrahamic covenant), the period of the law has come to an end (4:2 calls the law a guardian and a steward until the time appointed by the Father).

The reason for this end of the Mosaic covenant is because it was a covenant exclusive to the Jews (see the contrast in 4:25-26 between Jerusalem that now is and the Jerusalem above which is free). Further, the casting out of the bondwoman (who is Hagar, who stands for the present Jerusalem in bondage) means that God's dealing with Moses in the law cannot now be binding on the Galatians. Thus to accept circumcision is to bring one under obligation to keep the whole law (5:3). The law here must refer to the Mosaic dispensation which cannot now stand with the new situation brought by Christ.[2]

When Paul writes in Galatians 4:10 that he is afraid that they are falling back into bondage to beggarly elements (compare 4:9-10 with 4:3) by the observation of days, months, seasons and years, it is difficult to imagine that his words could have a positive attitude toward Sabbath-keeping. Any attempt to impose Sabbath-keeping or any of the other Jewish festivals on Gentiles is wrong.[3]

Colossians 2:16

The keeping of the Sabbath and other Jewish festivals are not wrong in themselves. Many Jewish believers continued to observe them (as did Paul when it helped in the preaching of the Gospel). Colossians 2:16 makes the point that no one should judge in matters of food, drink, festivals, new moons or sabbaths. These practices were only shadows of things to come. The substance is Christ. Believers may continue to enjoy and use these festivals, but their intrinsic value has been lost.[4] Thus Sabbaths are no longer binding on believers.

The Old Testament Law

But what is to be said of the Old Testament law? Is it not part of a believer's life? The Lord's Day view advocates that the Old Testament law must be properly interpreted in the light of the coming of Christ. Paul comments in 1 Corinthians 9:22 that he himself is not without law toward those who are under law, but rather he is under the law of Christ. It is not to be maintained, necessarily, that Paul is speaking of a new law for the church. This phrase could have relevance for the Sabbath if it could be shown that Jesus taught a particular attitude toward the Sabbath. But this phrase, "the law of Christ," in 1 Corinthians 9:22 does not refer to a body of Christian norms or laws. More likely it refers to a law of love which Paul elsewhere describes as the norm of his relationships.[5]

Furthermore, it is clear that because the Ten Commandments are a part of the Mosaic covenant, they are not necessarily binding on believers. If one wishes to use the phrase "the commandments of God" in 1 Corinthians 7:19 as a reference to the Ten Commandments in hopes of making these (including the Sabbath commandment) binding on New Testament believers, the Lord's Day view would argue that there is no evidence that it refers exclusively or primarily to the Ten Commandments. Plus the mention of circumcision in this same text as being nothing (while the keeping of the commandment is what matters) gives a good way to look at the Old Testament.

Although circumcision is not part of the decalogue, it was one of God's commandments. But it is no longer applicable to the believer. Circumcision is nothing because of the coming of Christ. The Old Testament law, including the Ten Commandments, must be applied in light of the coming of Christ. Keeping God's commandments means an obedience to the will of God disclosed in His Son.[6] Our starting point for applying the Old Testament must be Jesus Christ.

Conclusion

The conclusion must be that for Paul the Mosaic covenant has ended, and therefore so has the Sabbath commandment. Any attempt to interpret Pauline texts to favor the observance of a Sabbath commandment is a misinterpretation. The New Testament believer is not without commands, but they are all by or through the Lord Jesus Christ.

CHAPTER 24

THE LORD'S DAY VIEW

Sabbath Rest in Hebrews

With the coming of Jesus Christ, the kingdom of God has broken into history. Although the fullness of the kingdom awaits the second coming, the kingdom is now present. This idea is usually spoken of in terms of "now but not yet." The book of Hebrews displays this kind of "eschatological tension" and the implications in this New Testament book for the concept of rest are significant.

Hebrews 2:5-3:6 emphasizes the "now" aspect for it stresses the certainty of salvation because of Jesus Christ. Hebrews 3:7 begins to stress the "not yet" aspect because it emphasizes the fear of falling away. The concept of rest as developed in these passages of Hebrews partakes of the same "now but not yet" tension.[1]

Future Rest in Hebrews

The future or "not yet" part of rest is seen in the words and quotations of Old Testament passages the author of Hebrews uses. Psalm 95:11, which reads, "Unto whom I swore in my wrath that they should not enter into my rest," is one of the verses quoted. It brings an important Greek word into the discussion. The "rest" (katapausis) of Psalm 95:11 is the land of Canaan or possibly the sanctuary of the temple (see also Psalm 132). It was common in the exegesis of the Jewish rabbis to connect Deuteronomy 12:9, Psalm 95:11 and Psalm 132:14 and make them refer to the future world. Thus the author of Hebrews sees God's "rest" (katapausis) as the future and final resting place, probably associated with the heavenly promised land, the heavenly Jerusalem and the heavenly sanctuary. By linking Psalm 95:11 with Genesis 2:2 (see Hebrews 4:3, 4 and 5), the author gives the concept of rest (katapausis) a broader eschatological interpretation. God's rest goes all the way back to Genesis and is seen as a consummation of God's purposes for creation.[2]

Present Rest in Hebrews

But the rest (katapausis) in Hebrews is not only future, it is also a present reality for believers. The resting place that Israel never attained is still to come, but believers already have access to it through faith.

The setting of Hebrews 3:16-19 becomes important in this regard. The setting is probably Numbers 14 where Israel is not wandering in the wilderness, but is on the verge of entering the promised land. The parallel with the New Testament people of God is that both stand directly before the fulfillment of God's promises. This would indicate a present fulfillment of the rest.

Also the verb for "enter" in Hebrews 4:3 is in the present tense--we are entering into that rest. Furthermore, the "today" of Psalm 95 is applied to the present situation of believers.[3] Rordorf comments that the future blessing of salvation is proclaimed anew in the "today" ushered in by Jesus.[4]

Further confirmation of the present reality of rest is seen in Hebrews 4:9. The verse reads, "There remaineth therefore a rest of the people of God." In this verse another word for rest is used, the Greek word sabbatismos. This is its only use found in the New Testament and it is deliberately substituted for katapausis. Sabbatismos stresses the celebration that takes place on the Sabbath. But what is this celebration of Sabbath rest that still remains for the people of God (4:9)? Hebrews 4:10 specifies that it is to enter God's rest (katapausis) and to thereby cease from one's own works. Ceasing from our works is not a reference to a physical resting, but it has in mind our dead sinful works. Thus we discharge the duty of Sabbath observance by turning from our sinful works and exercising faith.[5]

The Nature of the Rest in Hebrews

The author of Hebrews does not have in mind a literal day or the Jewish Sabbath in this discussion of rest. With the coming of Jesus Christ the work of salvation is accomplished, but the new heavens and new earth has not yet dawned. The major question is how the New Testament writers see the Sabbath as fitting into this period before the complete fulfillment of God's rest.[6] The "rest" of the seventh day Sabbath is not transferred to the first day. With the fulfillment in Christ the old categories of the covenant are reinterpreted and transformed (Hebrews 8:13, 7:11-19, and 28 say that the first covenant is obsolete in light of the new covenant).

Thus the true Sabbath which has come with Christ is not a literal, physical rest, but it consists in the salvation God has provided in Christ. Thus there is no warrant in applying the physical rest of the Old Testament to the New Testament.[7] However, as Christians do meet together to worship on the Lord's Day, they will commemorate the true Sabbath rest because they are celebrating God's salvation.[8]

Continuity and Discontinuity in Hebrews

To carry the argument further, attention is called to the continuity (that which continues) and discontinuity (that which does not continue) clearly seen in the book of Hebrews between the old and new covenants. Continuity is seen in the fact that in both covenants God has spoken (1:1-2 and 3:2-6) and that the Old Testament is used by the author to communicate the Word of God into the new situation that believers in Christ face (see 2:6-8, 3:7-4:10, 10:37-38, chapter 11, 12:5-8, 13-17 and 13:5-6).

The discontinuity is seen in Christ's superiority to the angels, Moses and the priesthood. Thus the law declared by angels (2:2), mediated by faithful Moses (3:2ff) and administered by the Levitical priesthood (7:5-28) is demonstrated to be inferior and imperfect to God's new revelation in Christ.

The bridge between the old and new covenants is seen in the notion of fulfillment in Christ. The author of Hebrews is able to treat the old revelation and law as both God's Word to the Christian community in one place and as obsolete in another place (see especially 8:6-7, 13 and 10:8-10) because of what has taken place in Jesus Christ. When the author is stressing what God has accomplished in Christ in a final way for human salvation, then the old covenant and law are seen to be obsolete. But when the author sees that the believer must persevere in faith until the final consummation, then the Old Testament retains its usefulness and power for exhortation.

Thus Psalm 95 is used to exhort the believers with the need to strive to enter God's rest. However, God's rest is something already opened up by Christ and available to believers. Sabbath observance is now seen as an entry into God's rest as a believer ceases from his own works and trusts in God.[9]

Summary

To summarize this chapter, one should recall it has been pointed out that the writer of Hebrews spoke of a present rest as well as a future rest. The present rest is associated with what Christ has done for us in salvation in the reality of our ceasing from our works and entering into the full benefits of His salvation. The future rest is the final resting place, the one probably associated with the heavenly promised land, the heavenly Jerusalem and the heavenly sanctuary.

But it must be remembered that in none of this does the author have in mind a literal day or the Jewish Sabbath. There is no transference from a seventh day to a first day, for the present rest is unrelated to any literal day. Rather, again, Sabbath rest and Sabbath observance is seen as an entrance by a believer into God's rest by ceasing from one's own works and by trusting in God.

CHAPTER 25

THE LORD'S DAY VIEW

Sabbath and Sunday
in the History of the Church

This chapter on the Sabbath and Sunday in the history of the church can only be given a few brief remarks.

Sunday the Day of Worship
for the Early Church

Sunday was clearly the day on which the early church worshipped. However, Sunday was not a day of rest. No one in the Roman empire stopped work on Sunday until after Constantine.[1] Most believers, especially before the second century, worshipped on Sunday evening.[2] The early Christians knew nothing about a sanctity attached to Sunday after the pattern of the Jewish Sabbath.[3] From the second century the Sabbath is written off as a specifically Jewish institution.[4]

Possible Uncertainty
about the Sabbath Commandment

It is interesting to note that even though the early church had a high regard for the Ten Commandments, there is little emphasis on the first part of the Ten Commandments. This may show an uncertainty on how the Sabbath commandment is to be interpreted.[5] The Epistle of Barnabas is the only second century work to treat the Sabbath commandment as a part of the decalogue. Yet his intent is not to show that the Christian observance of Sunday is a fulfillment of the Sabbath commandment. The author interprets the Sabbath commandment to apply to holiness (not physical rest) and to apply to the future and final Sabbath that follows the second coming of Christ.[6]

A Later Metaphorical View of the Sabbath

In the second to fourth centuries a non-literal interpretation of the Sabbath becomes prominent. The literal command to rest one day in seven is seen to be a temporary ordinance for Israel alone. The sabbath commandment is a part of the Jewish ceremonial regulations. Further, the Sabbath commandment did not mean that we should abstain from work one day out of seven, but that the Christian should abstain at all times from every sinful act and thus devote every day to God.[7]

The Decree of Constantine

Sunday was not made a day of rest until Constantine became Emperor. However, even in Constantine's decree the Old Testament was not the foundation for Sunday legislation, but political and social considerations were far more influential.[8] In fact, it is striking that no church council refers to this imperial legislation concerning Sunday rest.[9] Prohibition of Sunday work is not found in any ecclesiastical legislation until the sixth century. The first author who claims any connection between the Sabbath and Sunday is Eusebius of Caeserea in his commentary on Psalm 92 (330 A.D.).[10]

Sunday Becomes the Christian Sabbath in the Middle Ages

A fully developed theology where the Sabbath regulations of the Old Testament are made applicable to Sunday does not occur until the Middle Ages. Two important concepts become prominent in this development. First, a distinction is made between the moral and ceremonial laws in specific reference to the Sabbath commandment, allowing for a literal application of the Sabbath commandment to Sunday. Second, the Ten Commandments are treated as natural law whereby all the moral precepts of the decalogue are also precepts of natural law.[11] These two developments become very important for subsequent history concerning the relationship between Sabbath and Sunday.

Summary

Thus we have seen that according to the Lord's Day view the concept of a Christian Sabbath was a very late development in the history of the church. The early church did worship on Sunday, but there was no concept of equating it with the Sabbath commandment or observing it as a day of rest. In the second to fourth centuries a view developed which saw physical rest as a temporary ordinance for Israel only and the Sabbath commandment as part of the Jewish ceremonial regulations. It was not till Constantine that Sunday was made a day of rest. The first church father to see any connection between the Sabbath and Sunday was Eusebius of Caeserea in 330 A.D. Finally, it was not until the Middle Ages that the Sabbath regulations of the Old Testament were made applicable to Sunday. Thus the transformation was complete and final.

CHAPTER 26

THE LORD'S DAY VIEW

Conclusions

D.A. Carson in his introduction to From Sabbath to Sunday sets forth several statements that will serve as a good summary of the Lord's Day view:

1. The New Testament does not develop a "transfer theology" where the Sabbath now moves to Sunday so that Sunday can be called the Christian Sabbath.

2. Sabbath-keeping is not presented in the Old Testament as the norm for creation.

3. The New Testament does not develop a pattern of continuity and discontinuity with the Old Testament on the basis of moral/civil ceremonial distinctions.

4. Sunday worship arose in New Testament times (not the second century), but it was not perceived as a Christian Sabbath.[1]

Similarities between the Sabbath and the Lord's Day

Further, although Sunday is the new day for worship and the Sabbath commandment does not apply to it, there still remains an analogy or similarities between the Sabbath and the Lord's Day. The first similarity is seen in the fact that both stress weekly worship. This does not necessarily mean that the Old Testament principle of one day in seven still continues today so that the Christians are to observe the whole day in a distinctive way. Yet the weekly interval for worship would naturally have suggested itself.[2]

A second similarity is seen in the notion of rest. This rest was part of redemption. The Sabbath was the memorial of redemption and the resurrection was the climax of God's redemption in Christ. The resurrection was also the fulfillment of the concept of rest. Worship on the Lord's Day is a participation of true Sabbath rest. The present enjoyment of this rest is a foretaste and guarantee of the future consummation rest.[3]

A third and final similarity between the Sabbath and Sunday is their relation to the concept of lordship. The Sabbath was "to the Lord" and can be called justifiably the Old Testament's Lord's Day where God's people worship Christ as Lord. On the Sabbath lordship was acknowledged by ceasing from work the whole day, but on Sunday lordship is proclaimed by meeting for worship a part of the day.[4]

Worship Not Physical Rest
the Priority of the Lord's Day

As has been stated several times through these chapters on the Lord's Day view, physical rest, which was a major part of the Sabbath commandment, is no longer a necessary part of Sunday. In other words, there is no Biblical or compelling theological reason why rest has to take place on Sunday. The need for physical rest is still very important. We share this concern for regular periods of rest for ourselves and others in society.[5] Sunday does allow most people in our society to both worship and rest. Although we should be thankful for this we should be careful not to build any theological edifice upon this convenient but accidental fact that we can both rest and worship on Sunday.[6]

Thus the priority for the Lord's Day is worship. In worship the church recognizes its Lord and all that "Christ is Lord" means for the church's existence. If worship is the "church's heartbeat" in this way, and if Sunday is the correct day for worship, then our attention and energy will not be directed so much as to what we should or should not do during the day, but how we can make sure that Sunday has the vitality and significance it should have.[7]

Summary

Though there are similarities between the Sabbath and the Lord's day, as noted above, there are also major distinctions. The Lord's day is not the Christian Sabbath. The Lord's Day does not require physical rest. The Lord's day finds its highest priority in worship. The Lord's Day should not cause us so much to question ourselves concerning do's and don'ts for that day, but it should cause us to ask how we can best use it in the worship of our God.

PART FOUR

A COMPARISON OF VIEWS

CHAPTER 27

A COMPARISON OF VIEWS

By now the reader has been introduced to all three of the major views of the subject of Sabbath/Sunday worship. Perhaps, however, the distinctions between the three views may be in need of summary and comparison in order to further acquaint and establish the convictions of each position in the reader's mind. Such a comparison will now be presented considering a number of the key issues in the discussion and disagreement.

I. THE SABBATH AT CREATION

A. The Seventh Day View

The Sabbath was established by God at creation as a creation ordinance, which means it is to be permanently observed by man. Sabbath observance is taught in Genesis 1-2, not by divine command, but by divine example. Moses in Exodus 20:11 traces Sabbath observance back to creation and records clearly that it was sanctified by God.

B. The Christian Sabbath View

The Sabbath was established by God at creation as a creation ordinance. Though not spelled out explicitly by direct command in the Biblical record to be a creation ordinance, there is enough evidence to lead to that conclusion. That evidence would include God's creation rest and the presence of a seven day week in the history of man. Later testimony of Scripture declares that God sanctified the Sabbath at creation.

C. The Lord's Day View

No evidence nor even a hint of evidence exists to say that the Sabbath was established as a creation ordinance in Genesis 2. God does rest on the seventh day following His work of creation, and God does bless and sanctify the day, but no mention is made here of a Sabbath for man, neither is there any command for man to keep the Sabbath. The rest of the seventh day centers solely on God and not on man.

II. THE SABBATH IN THE MOSAIC LAW

A. The Seventh Day View

The Sabbath has a strong and important place in the Mosaic covenant. It is one of the Ten Commandments. It is a sign of the Mosaic covenant. It demonstrated Israel's love and fear of God. It speaks strongly of redemption and liberation whereby man is then able to give selfless, compassionate service to God and others.

B. The Christian Sabbath View

The Sabbath has stood from creation as God's requirement of man. At the giving of the Law at Mt. Sinai, its permanence is further established as it was made part of the moral law, the Ten Commandments. Because of this, it continues as a moral imperative for the church today. However, Sabbath observance is not mandated for the seventh day, which conviction sets it apart from the Seventh Day view.

C. The Lord's Day View

The establishment of the Sabbath in the Mosaic covenant was not based on any creation ordinance given in Genesis. Neither is it based on the Noahic covenant. Rather, the Sabbath originated at Mt. Sinai and is based on the previous historical event of Israel's deliverance from Egypt. It was a sign of the Mosaic covenant, and was given to Israel only, and lasted only for the duration of that Old Testament covenant.

III. THE SABBATH IN THE TEACHINGS OF CHRIST

A. The Seventh Day View

Christ is the fulfillment of the Sabbath promises which were given at creation, and the blessings He brings are also the fulfillment of the Sabbath promises. But this does not mean He did away with the Sabbath. Rather He established it. There is no evidence in His teachings or example that He desired or tried to establish another day besides the seventh as the proper day of worship. He never alluded to any other day of worship. He never observed another day of worship. He was in controversy about the proper use and observance of the Sabbath, but He never hinted that the Sabbath observances were trivial because they would be replaced by a new day of worship. He took for granted the permanence of the Sabbath in His teachings. He even indicated that He is Lord of the Sabbath. He clearly sought to uphold the Sabbath and its proper function in agreement with the fourth commandment.

B. The Christian Sabbath View

Jesus never gave any indication that the Sabbath was abolished with His coming or that it would be eliminated after His death, resurrection and ascension. His controversies over the Sabbath with the religious leaders of His day were not over Sabbath observance itself, but over the Pharisaical interpretations of it. He did appear to place the Sabbath in the category of moral law as He treated it differently than the ceremonial regulations. The basis for a change from the seventh day to the first day of the week for Sabbath observance is based on His Lordship and the fact He was raised from the dead the first day of the week.

C.   The Lord's Day View

There is no evidence that Jesus was committed in practice or belief to the Sabbath as the necessary day of worship. His habit of synagogue attendance was merely an opportunity to minister. Some of His statements and practices indicate He had power to transcend the Sabbath. His attitude was that the law, including the Sabbath, has been replaced by His authority and teaching. He transcends the law. The demands of the law remain in force only within His teachings. In some cases He will affirm the law, and in other cases, such as the Sabbath, He will disaffirm it.

IV.   THE SABBATH TEACHINGS IN PAUL

A.   The Seventh Day View

Though some would argue to the contrary, using certain Pauline texts, this view is convinced there is no evidence in Paul's writings or life that would indicate he encouraged or taught an elimination of the Sabbath or the introduction of the first day as the day of worship. In those passages, which some would use to argue to the contrary, Paul was simply writing to correct some abuse or abuses of the Sabbath. One should not use verses written to correct such abuses to set aside the Sabbath altogether.

B.   The Christian Sabbath View

No passage in the writings of Paul, which seem to negate or allow the negation of certain days, not even Colossians 2:16-17 nor Romans 14:4, has in view the Christian Sabbath, though these passages may refer to Jewish Sabbaths. The reason the Christian Sabbath is not to be included in these passages is because the Jewish regulations about the Sabbath had degenerated to little more than legalistic ceremonialism. This abuse is what Paul rejects in such passages--that is, the misinterpretations of the true Jewish Sabbath.

C.   The Lord's Day View

For Paul the Mosaic covenant had ended, which meant that the Sabbath command had ended also. Any attempt to interpret the Pauline statements, such as Galatians 3:6 and Colossians 2:16, as favoring the observance of a Sabbath command is a misinterpretation. The New Testament believer is not without commands, but they are all by and through the Lord Jesus Christ. He never set forth such a Sabbath command.

V.   THE SABBATH IN RELATION TO MORAL AND CEREMONIAL LAW

A.   The Seventh Day View

Any argument that says the Sabbath command in the Ten Commandments is set aside for us today because it is part of the ceremonial law is inconsistent. Why, then, does not one have the same attitude towards the rest of the other Ten Commandments? How can the Sabbath commandment be both ceremonial and moral? Some seem to contend it is ceremonial in that it specifies the Seventh day, but it is moral for setting apart a day of rest for worship. But if one rejects the Seventh day Sabbath as the day of worship because it is supposedly ceremonial, does that not also destroy the moral basis for worshipping God on one day at all?

B.   The Christian Sabbath View

The Christian is free from the law in the sense that the law is not observed as a means of salvation. However, the law still has a positive effect in the life of the believer. Keeping the commandments of God's moral law is still very important. Since the fourth commandment is one of the Ten Commandments (the moral law), keeping the Sabbath command is important also. Yet the form of the law in the New Testament is different than in the Old Testament for in the New Testament covenant the law is written in the believer's heart. Full blessedness is a result of obedience to God's law, while believers who live unrighteously are chastened by the Lord.

C.   The Lord's Day View

The Sabbath is seen as being part of the ceremonial law and not the moral law. Thus the Sabbath is no longer binding on the believer.

VI.   THE SABBATH REST OF HEBREWS

A.   The Seventh Day View

Hebrews 4 refutes the idea that the blessings of Sabbath-keeping were tied to the Jewish national covenant. This section of Scripture (chapters 3-4) argues that another Sabbath rest remains for the people of God. The author seeks to move the Jews addressed away from the exclusive and material view of the Sabbath, and to establish its universal, redemptive and spiritual nature. To do this the author traces the origin of Sabbath rest back to creation, and stresses that Sabbath rest must be entered now. All of this is related to and anchored in actual present Sabbath observance and not just looking to the fulfillment of Sabbath blessings in the future.

B.   The Christian Sabbath View

Hebrews 3:7-4:13 rests on the assumption that believers in the new covenant are in a similar situation as Israel in the wilderness. Both are given the promise of rest. Both are exposed to trials and the danger of unbelief. Both are exhorted to persevere in faith. This rest of the church today is entirely future, coming at Christ's return. The eschatological benefits of salvation are present today, but the rest is not. The rest in Hebrews 3-4, because it is entirely future, implies the weekly Sabbath still remains in force under the new covenant. Further, the fact that the rest in

Hebrews 3-4 is grounded in God's rest at creation supports the idea that the weekly Sabbath is a creation ordinance. Therefore, there is a Christian Sabbath.

C. The Lord's Day View

The writer of Hebrews spoke of a present rest as well as a future rest. The present rest is associated with what Christ has done for us in salvation and is fulfilled in us as we cease from our sinful works and enter into the full benefits of His salvation. The future rest is the final rest associated with eternity. None of this necessitates or establishes a literal day or the Jewish Sabbath.

VII. THE SABBATH IN APOSTOLIC EXAMPLE

A. The Seventh Day View

There is no evidence in the apostolic church that the believers of that day worshipped on Sunday. The gathering of believers in Acts 20:7 was not a normal gathering, but a special meeting for the departure of Paul. 1 Corinthians 16:1-2 says nothing about an assembling of believers, but records instructions given to individuals to carry out at home. When Revelation 1:10 speaks of the Lord's Day, it is a reference to the coming future day of the Lord and does not refer to Sunday as the Lord's Day. Finally, although the resurrection of Christ was a very important event, no connection is made in the New Testament between worship on Sunday and the event of the resurrection.

B. The Christian Sabbath View

The resurrection is the most momentous event in history and gives reason and justification for the change of the day of worship. The recorded resurrection appearances of Christ all take place on Sunday. Furthermore, Acts 20:7 is a Sunday evening worship service. 1 Corinthians 16:1-2 contains instructions given to the church as a congregation. Revelation 1:10 is a clear reference to Sunday as the Lord's Day. This evidence of apostolic practice is authoritative for us today.

C.   The Lord's Day View

Although the evidence is scarce, what we do possess, when taken together as a whole, points toward the fact that Sunday is the Lord's Day. The clearest passage is Revelation 1:10, which is identified as showing Sunday is the Lord's Day. Although the resurrection appearances of Christ on Sunday and Acts 20:7 and 1 Corinthians 16:1-2 are not absolutely conclusive, they also add to the weight of the evidence, especially in light of the practices of the second-century church.

VIII. THE SABBATH AND THE LORD'S DAY

A.   The Seventh Day View

The only possible reference to a supposed Lord's Day is Revelation 1:10. To see this as an established day of worship on the first day of the week is to read the second century evidence of the Church fathers back into the first century. It is better to see this phrase as a reference to the coming day of the Lord.

B.   The Christian Sabbath View

The term "Lord's Day" is a unique expression in the New Testament which shows that one day of the week, not every day, is special to the Lord. This special day, the Lord's Day, is a continuation of the Sabbath and should be considered essentially one and the same institution. This Lord's Day is the Christian Sabbath. It is the day the early church proclaimed Jesus as Lord.

C. The Lord's Day View

The phrase "the Lord's Day" is found in one Biblical reference, Revelation 1:10. It was the first day of the week, the day of Christ's resurrection, and the day Christians worshipped. But it was not related to the Sabbath commandment of the Mosaic law, neither was it a literal day of rest.

IX. THE SABBATH IN THE POST-APOSTOLIC PERIOD

A. The Seventh Day View

Sunday worship did not arise in the Jerusalem Church, because this was obviously a Jewish church, and such a change would have been unthinkable. Rather, Sunday worship rose in a community of Gentile believers, probably at Rome, when for various reasons, the church was trying to make a break with Judaism. Therefore it is concluded that Sunday observance does not rest on a foundation of Biblical truth or apostolic authority, but on the efforts of the second century church.

B. The Christian Sabbath View

Early in the history of the church, a theology of the Lord's Day arose. It included the concept of a whole day, the first day, to be set aside for the Lord. It was a holy day set aside for worship and remembrance of Christ and His blessings, and also it was to be a day of rest. It was the Christian Sabbath.

C. The Lord's Day View

Evidence concerning the origin of Sunday worship in the history of the church is scarce. Maybe Sunday worship rose from the resurrection appearances of Christ which took place on Sunday. Maybe Sunday worship originated in the

Palestinian Jewish/Christian churches. Whatever the case, in early church history, when Christians needed a time for distinctly Christian worship, Sunday was established as a commemoration of Christ's resurrection. In this establishment there was no relation between this new day of worship and the Sabbath commandment of the Old Testament.

X.   THE SABBATH AND PRACTICAL CONSIDERATIONS

A.   The Seventh Day View

The Sabbath is certainly important to the needs and problems of modern man. Man needs the weekly, divinely-centered rest provided by the Sabbath. Such not only is a benefit physically and spiritually, but it is also an expression of our complete commitment to God. It also acknowledges God as the authority over this world and that He will make us better caretakers of it for Him.

B.   The Christian Sabbath View

Those holding to the Christian Sabbath are not agreed on all matters pertaining to its practical application. All agree as to the need of observance and respect for the first day of the week. All agree it should be a day of worship and rest. But there is a concern that in making practical application that one steer a proper course between legalism and lawlessness. The place of the government in relation to enforcement is also a point of disagreement. Some favor the government recognizing a day and even establishing blue laws, particularly the older commentators. The other commentators do not necessarily desire governmental recognition or the establishment of blue laws.

C. The Lord's Day View

One of the most important practical aspects of the Lord's Day view is that physical rest, which is connected with the Old Testament, has no necessity in Lord's Day observance. Man needs rest, and we can be grateful that in our society our day of worship can be used as a day of rest. But this physical rest for us today is not connected to nor necessitated by the Old Testament Sabbath commandment. What is truly important on the Lord's Day is making worship a priority.

Other subject areas and Scripture verses could be summarized under each of the three views we have considered, but those chosen should be sufficient to help the reader finalize an understanding of the distinctions and differences.

CONCLUSION

The result of this work in the lives of the readers may be three-fold. For some, it has further established a conviction already held. For others, it may have raised issues and questions which still need to be resolved. For even a few, perhaps, it has changed your previous convictions.

Whatever the reaction of the readers, the authors of this work before concluding wish to set forth several principles of encouragement and instruction.

1. A Difficult Subject

The reader is encouraged to recognize that we have been dealing with a very difficult subject which is composed of some extremely difficult issues. This is not to say that the authors do not have a viewpoint of their own on the subject. Hopefully in the future, they intend to present their position which will set forth their own exegesis and arguments. But for now we urge the reader to admit the difficulty and complexity of the subject which has been discussed.

2. Further Study Is Needed

The reader is encouraged to study the matter further and come to a firm conviction. If it is asked, how can one make a decision on such a difficult subject, the following suggestions are set forth for guidance.

First, one key to the subject matter is whether or not the Sabbath is a creation ordinance. True, there is no command in Genesis for mankind to observe the Sabbath. There is no record man observed the Sabbath in Genesis. Also there is no record of the necessity of Sabbath observance in the Noahic covenant. The question that must be answered then is whether or not God's example in Genesis is to be man's practice, and whether later Scripture teaches the Sabbath was set apart and sanctified for man at creation. Even if this be so, does it mean it is a creation ordinance?

Second, another key to the determination of one's conviction is the place of the Mosaic law, specifically the Ten Commandments, in the life of a believer. Particularly, is the fourth commandment to be considered a part of the moral law or is it merely ceremonial law? Even more basic, is the moral/ceremonial distinction a valid distinction in reference to the law or more particularly to the Ten Commandments? How significant is it that the Sabbath is a sign of the Mosaic covenant, and what are the implications for the Sabbath when the New Covenant comes? Does the Sabbath then continue as it was observed in the Old Testament, or does the Sabbath transfer its obligations and practices to a new day, or is the Sabbath replaced by a new day with no connection to the fourth commandment.

Third, of great importance is Christ's view of the Sabbath. What are the implications of the fact that He observed the Jewish Sabbath? Did Christ's Sabbath controversies relate primarily to the Jewish misinterpretations of the Sabbath law or did they give a ground to make a change concerning the Sabbath day and its practices. How significant is the resurrection?

Fourth, another important piece of the puzzle concerns how the apostles, with special reference to Paul, taught concerning the Sabbath. How does one handle the negative remarks that Paul seems to make concerning the Sabbath? Is he talking about the Sabbath at all in these passages? How much significance in establishing a practice should be given to the resurrection appearances of Christ on the first day of the week? How strong a foundation is laid for apostolic example and even apostolic command for Sunday worship from Acts 20:7, 1 Corinthians 16:1-2 and Revelation 1:10?

Fifth, a final area of study and concern, though not as essential as the above areas related to Scripture, would be the testimony of church history. This area is very difficult. In some areas of theology and practices the post-apostolic church very quickly left the beliefs and practices of the apostles. Further, it is difficult to establish firm conclusions when very few church fathers comment on a subject. One needs to be careful not to draw an argument from silence. The difficulty of using church history in the argument is recognized by Rordorf when he admits that he and Bacchiocchi come to exact opposite positions even while using the same historical evidence.[1] The writers urge the readers to consult church history, but not to draw conclusions solely on that basis.

3. A Plea for Unity

Finally, there is sent forth a plea for unity in the body of Christ even though there exists a difference of conviction on the subject. Not only is there a difference between various theological traditions, but there is disagreement among those within the same theological tradition. Whether it be Baptists or Presbyterians or even some other group (though not every group), there is disagreement. One author admits that there is a family quarrel of long-standing within the Reformed tradition. Two different meanings of the Sabbath commandment flow to the Reformed community today from two different standards of faith, the Heidelberg Catechism and the Westminster Confession.[2]

In stressing unity it is recognized that the Lord's Day view is more conducive to an attitude of unity than the other two views. Or to turn the matter around, the Seventh Day view and the Christian Sabbath view might find it more difficult to join in a spirit of unity. But it should be possible for each to treat the others in a brotherly spirit of love and kindness, even though there are distinctions of convictions, and even though there is a desire to maintain and uphold those distinctions in separate churches and denominations.

Third, though a plea for unity goes forth to the reader, it is not a unity at any price which is advocated. Certain theological positions regarding this subject of the day of worship are Biblically out-of-bounds. For example, the keeping of a particular day of worship, Saturday or Sunday, or how that day is to be observed, can never become a part of the means of obtaining right standing before God. The day of worship has nothing to do with justification as justification is by faith alone.

Another conviction or attitude which must be rejected is the thought that observing a certain day can add to one's holiness or sanctification. The practices which are required or the restrictions which are demanded should not be seen as means to promote one's own self-righteousness.

Can the reader deny these final conclusions which have been stated concerning the Sabbath question? Let them be stated in one sentence. The Sabbath question is a difficult subject which requires careful study and a heart, which when persuaded, holds its conviction firmly, yet with a spirit of unity towards others who may disagree.

ENDNOTES

Introduction

[1]D. A. Carson, "Introduction," From Sabbath to Lord's Day (Grand Rapids: Zondervan Publishing House, 1982), pp. 16-17 comments on some of these issues.

Chapter 1

[1]Samuele Bacchiocchi, From Sabbath to Sunday (Rome: Pontifical Gregorian University Press, 1977), p. 310.

[2]Bacchiocchi, Divine Rest for Human Restlessness (Rome: Pontifical Gregorian University Press, 1980), p. 20.

[3]Ibid., pp. 20-22.

[4]Ibid., p. 81.

[5]Ibid., Sabbath, p. 21.

[6]Ibid., Divine Rest, pp. 83-84.

[7]Ibid., pp. 90-91.

[8]Ibid., p. 57. Bacchiocchi notes that in Hellenistic Judaism the Sabbath was viewed as a creation ordinance for mankind. However, the Palestinian rabbis reduced the Sabbath from a creation ordinance to a Mosaic ordinance exclusively for Israel due to pressures to abandon the Jewish religion (Ibid., p. 33).

[9]Ibid., p. 62.

[10]Ibid., p. 34.

[11]Ibid.

[12]Ibid., pp. 34-35.

[13]Ibid., Sabbath, p. 28 note 33 where Bacchiocchi gives the Jewish references.

[14]Ibid., Divine Rest, pp. 35-36.

Chapter 2

[1]Bacchiocchi, Divine Rest, pp. 35-36.

[2]Ibid., p. 113.

[3]Ibid., pp. 140-141.

[4]Ibid., Sabbath, pp. 318-319.

[5]Ibid., Divine Rest, 141-142.

[6]Ibid., p. 137.

[7]Ibid., p. 142.

[8]Ibid., Sabbath, p. 23.

Chapter 3

[1]Ibid., Sabbath, p. 21.

[2]Ibid., Divine Rest, p. 148.

[3]Ibid., p. 134.

[4]Ibid., Sabbath, p. 26.

[5]Ibid., p. 35. In Matthew 11 Christ offers rest and an easy yoke. The yoke is the law, but it is not burdensome because the believer does not submit himself to a new set of rules but to Christ himself. The law to a believer expresses a special relationship to God (Good News, pp. 162-163).

[6]Ibid., Sabbath, pp. 52-54.

[7]Ibid., pp. 32 and 47.

[8]Ibid., p. 61.

[9]Ibid., Divine Rest, p. 160.

[10]Ibid., Sabbath, p. 56. Bacchiocchi notes that Mark 2:27-28 should be seen in parallel with Matthew 19:8, where Christ traces both the Sabbath and marriage back to creation to clarify their fundamental value and function for humanity (Divine Rest, p. 41).

[11]Ibid., Sabbath, pp. 38-39 and 41.

[12]Ibid., p. 44.

[13]Ibid., p. 48, footnote 83.

[14]Ibid., p. 38.

[15]Ibid., p. 26, footnote 25.

[16]Ibid., p. 71. Bacchiocchi comments that Mark omits the statement concerning flight on the Sabbath because he was writing to a different audience which was not impeded by Jewish restrictions (p. 70).

[17]Ibid., p. 72.

[18]Ibid., p. 19, footnote 6.

Chapter 4

[1]Ibid., pp. 63-64.

[2]Ibid.

[3]Ibid., pp. 64-65.

[4]Ibid., Divine Rest, pp. 169-170.

[5]Ibid., Sabbath, p. 65.

[6]Ibid., Divine Rest, p. 166.

[7]Ibid., Sabbath, p. 65.

[8]Bacchiocchi notes that the majority of commentators interprets the Sabbath rest in Hebrews 4 as an exclusively future rest and so have failed to grasp the implications of the exhortation for its present observance (Sabbath, pp. 65-67).

[9]Ibid., Divine Rest, pp. 135-136.

[10]Although the verbs in 4:7 are aorist (past tense), they have the force of indicating an experience in the past which continues to be present, in Bacchiocchi's view. The Revised Standard Version translates both verbs with the present tense (Sabbath, p. 67).

[11]Ibid., Sabbath, p. 68. Bacchiocchi recognizes that Christ has brought about a "decisive discontinuity" (a radical break with the past) concerning the sacrificial system of the Old Covenant (Hebrews 7-10). Hebrews 8:5 says that the Old Covenant is a copy and shadow. Hebrews 10:9 says it is abolished. Hebrews 8:13 says it is obsolete and ready to pass away. He then asks whether the Sabbath is in the same category. His answer is "no" because a Sabbath rest still remains for the people of God (Divine Rest, pp. 166-167).

Chapter 5

[1]Ibid., Sabbath, p. 150.

[2]Ibid., p. 339.

[3]Ibid., pp. 339-340.

[4]Ibid., pp. 348-350. The Greek word "cheirographon" also occurs in Ephesians 2:15. Bacchiocchi tries to show that Colossians 2 and

Ephesians 2 are very different so that "cheirographon" does not mean the same in the two passages.

[5]The view that "sabbaths" includes the Sabbath day is in opposition to the traditional Seventh-Day Adventist interpretation where it is denied that "sabbaths" refers to the weekly Sabbath (<u>Sabbath</u>, p. 359).

[6]Ibid., p. 352.

[7]Ibid., pp. 344-345.

[8]Ibid., pp. 346-347.

[9]Ibid., pp. 345-346.

[10]Ibid., p. 355.

[11]Ibid., pp. 356-357 and p. 359.

[12]Ibid., p. 365.

[13]Ibid., p. 367.

[14]Ibid., p. 364.

[15]Ibid., p. 358.

Chapter 6

[1]Ibid., p. 13.

[2]Ibid., pp. 142-143. Bacchiocchi notes that the Apostolic Council in Acts 15 (58 A. D.) shows how attached the Jerusalem church was to the customs of Moses. Exemption from circumcision was granted only to the Gentiles. On other matters related to the law (ritual defilement and food laws), Gentiles were not granted complete freedom. Thus there was great respect shown for the ceremonial law. The fact that it is mentioned that the law of Moses is read in the synagogue every

Sabbath completely excludes the hypothesis that the Sabbath had been replaced by Sunday (Ibid., pp. 146-150).

[3]Ibid., p. 136.

[4]Ibid., p. 151.

[5]Ibid., p. 153.

[6]The curse was: "May the apostate have not any hope and may the empire of pride be uprooted promptly in our days. May the Nazarenes and the Minim perish in an instant, may they be erased from the book of life, that they may not be counted among the righteous. Blessed be Thou, O God, who bringest down the proud." Bacchiocchi comments that cursing the Christians under the name "Nazarene" was probably not just to pronounce them as apostates, but also to discover if any were in the synagogue (Ibid., p. 158).

[7]Ibid., pp. 158-159. After Hadrian put down the Barkokeba revolt (132-135 A. D.), he built a new Roman city on the ruins of Jerusalem and imposed harsh restrictions on the Jewish people, including the prohibition of circumcision and the Sabbath.

[8]Ibid., p. 165.

[9]Ibid., pp. 165-169.

[10]Ibid., pp. 170-171 and 174.

[11]Ibid., pp. 178 and 183.

[12]Ibid., p. 186.

[13]Ibid., p. 235. Besides the controversy between the Christians and the Jews, Bacchiocchi gives other factors that he believes lead to the adoption of Sunday worship. Even though anti-Jewish attitudes created the necessity for a new day of worship, it did not determine the specific choice of Sunday. The influence of Sun-worship with its Sun-day may provide a plausible explanation for the Christian choice of Sunday as a day of worship (Ibid., pp. 236-237).

[14]Ibid., p. 306.

15Ibid., p. 309. Bacchiocchi states that Protestants who base their practices and beliefs solely on the authority of Scripture find themselves in an apparent contradiction concerning the observance of Sunday since it is based on the tradition of the church instead of the authority of Scripture.

Chapter 7

1Ibid., p. 10.

2Willy Rordorf in the book Sunday, trans. by A. A. Grahm (Philadelphia: Westminster Press, 1968) divorces rest from worship.

3Bacchiocchi, Sabbath, p. 317.

4Ibid., p. 318.

5Ibid., pp. 318-319.

6Ibid., Divine Rest, p. 93.

7Ibid., Sabbath, p. 320.

8Ibid., Divine Rest, pp. 68-69.

9Ibid., p. 76.

10Ibid., pp. 102-103.

11Ibid., p. 185.

12Ibid., pp. 175 and 177-178.

13Ibid., p. 186. Bacchiocchi warns of the danger of trying to make certain Sabbath activities lawful or unlawful. Such an approach leads to legalistic attitudes which stifle freedom and creativity. However, he lists three criteria one could use to evaluate Sabbath activities. First, Sabbath activities should be God-centered and not self-centered. Second, they should bring freedom and joy. Third, they should be recreative in the sense that they restore physical, emotional and mental energies (Ibid., pp. 202-203).

[14]Ibid., pp. 207 and 209.

[15]Ibid., pp. 209-210 and 212-213.

[16]Ibid., p. 19.

Chapter 8

[1]Ibid., Sabbath, p. 75.

[2]Ibid., pp. 270-271.

[3]Ibid., p. 316. Bacchiocchi comments that the fact that the Passover was observed by the fixed date of Nisan 15, regardless of the day, makes it untenable that Christ's resurrection determined the origin of Sunday worship during the lifetime of the apostles (Sabbath, p. 84).

[4]Ibid., p. 63.

[5]Ibid., Divine Rest, p. 225.

[6]Ibid., Sabbath, pp. 86-87.

[7]Ibid., pp. 103-104.

[8]Ibid., pp. 106-107. Bacchiocchi also argues that the phrase "to break bread" did not become a technical term for the Lord's Supper until later. Of the fifteen times it occurs in the New Testament, nine times it is used of Christ (feeding the multitude, the Last Supper and eating with the disciples after the resurrection), two times of Paul eating a meal, two times of the breaking of bread in the Lord's Supper and two times of believers breaking bread together. Just because the phrase "to break bread" occurs does not necessarily indicate a reference to the Lord's Supper (Sabbath, pp. 108-109).

[9]Ibid., pp. 102 and 107.

[10]Ibid., p. 111.

[11]Ibid., p. 100.

[12]Ibid., pp. 93-94.

[13]Ibid., p. 113.

[14]Ibid., p. 17, footnote 1.

[15]Ibid., p. 117.

[16]Ibid., p. 118.

[17]Ibid., pp. 124-127.

[18]Bacchiocchi states that it was not until late medieval theology (Thomas Aquinas) that the literal application of the Sabbath commandment was made to Sunday. This application was made possible by a new view which distinguished between a moral and ceremonial aspect of the Sabbath commandment and the law in general. The moral aspect was said to be grounded in Natural Law (Ibid., Divine Rest, p. 45).

[19]Ibid., Divine Rest, pp. 45-46.

[20]See Rordorf, Sunday, p. 298.

Chapter 9

[1]Richard B. Gaffin, Jr., "A Sabbath Rest Still Awaits the People of God," Pressing Toward the Mark, ed. by Charles G. Dennison and Richard C. Gamble (Philadelphia: Committee for the Historian of the Orthodox Presbyterian Church, 1986), p. 47.

[2]John Murray, Principles of Conduct (Grand Rapids: William B. Eerdmans Publishing Co., 1957), pp. 30-31.

3O. Palmer Robertson, The Christ of the Covenants (Phillipsburg, NJ: Presbyterian and Reformed Publishing Co., 1980), pp. 68-69.

4Robert G. Rayburn, "Should Christians Observe the Sabbath?" Presbyterion, 10 (Spring-Fall 1984):73.

5John Murray recognizes the possibility that the seventh day which was blessed at creation was not the seventh day in our weekly cycle but the seventh day in the sphere of God's creation. Whichever view one may take, he believes the inference is inevitable that God blessed and sanctified the seventh day in our week because he sanctified the seventh day in his own realm of creative activity. See Principles of Conduct, p. 31.

6Murray, "The Moral Law and the Fourth Commandment," The Claims of Truth (Carlisle, PA: Banner of Truth Trust, 1976), p. 207.

7Murray, Principles of Conduct, pp. 32-34.

8Robertson, Christ of the Covenants, pp. 68-69.

9Murray, Principles of Conduct, p. 27.

10J. O. Peck, "The Sabbath a Necessity to All Forms of Social Regeneration," Sabbath Essays, ed. by Will C. Wood (Boston: Congregational Society, 1880), p. 49.

11Some see a reference to Sabbath observance in the phrase "at the end of days" in Genesis 4:3. The phrase speaks of when Cain and Abel brought their offering to the Lord (See Francis N. Lee, The Covenantal Sabbath [London: Lord's Day Observance Society, n. d.], pp. 84-85).

12Gerhardus Vos, Biblical Theology (Grand Rapids: William B. Eerdmans Publishing Co., 1948), p. 155.

13Gaffin, "Sabbath Rest," p. 51, footnote 37.

14Joshua Tucker, "The Pre-Mosaic Sabbath," Sabbath Essays, pp. 192-193.

[15]Murray, Principles of Conduct, p. 35.

[16]Roger T. Beckwith and Wilfred Stott, The Christian Sunday (Grand Rapids: Baker Book House, 1978), p. 4.

[17]Ibid., p. 146, footnote 4 where the authors assert that the Sabbath so controls the biblical week that it at times is used as one of the names for the week (as in Leviticus 23:15 and 25:8).

[18]Charles Hodge, Systematic Theology, 3 vols. (Grand Rapids: William B. Eerdmans Publishing Co., 1952), 3:328.

[19]Robertson, Christ of the Covenants, pp. 68-69.

Chapter 10

[1]Beckwith, Christian Sunday, pp. 4-5.

[2]Ibid.

[3]Vos, Biblical Theology, p. 155.

[4]Paul G. Schrotenboer, Acts of the Reformed Ecumenical Synod (Grand Rapids: Reformed Ecumenical Synod Secretariat, 1972), p. 159.

[5]Gordon H. Clark, What Presbyterians Believe (Philadelphia: Presbyterian and Reformed Publishing Co., 1965), pp. 181-182.

[6]Hodge, Systematic Theology, 3:322.

[7]Beckwith, Christian Sunday, pp. 44-45.

[8]The terms "memorial of creation" and "memorial of redemption" are used by Beckwith in Christian Sunday.

[9]Ibid., pp. 14-15.

[10]Hodge, Systematic Theology, 3:323.

[11]Ibid.

[12]G. I. Williamson, The Westminster Confession of Faith for Study Classes (Philadelphia: Presbyterian and Reformed Publishing Co., 1964), pp. 142-143.

[13]Hodge, Systematic Theology, 3:324.

[14]Rayburn, "Should Christians Observe?", p. 75.

[15]Hodge, Systematic Theology, 3:323 and 329.

[16]Rayburn, "Should Christians Observe?", p. 77.

[17]Clark, What Presbyterians Believe, p. 201.

[18]Rayburn, "Should Christians Observe?", p. 72.

[19]Robertson, Christ of the Covenants, pp. 70-74 shows how a Sabbath principle manifested itself in a variety of ways in the Old Testament, including the Sabbath and Jubilee years, the years of exile and even future expectations. Thus it appears that the Sabbath principle structures history.

[20]Hodge, Systematic Theology, 3:325.

Chapter 11

[1]Rayburn, "Should Christians Observe?", p. 79.

[2]Robert Reymond, "The Lord's Day Observance: Man's Proper Response to the Fourth Commandment," Presbyterion, 13 (Spring 1987):17-19.

[3]Murray, "Moral Law," p. 221.

[4]Luke 4:16 mentions that it was Jesus' custom to go to the synagogue.

[5]Archibald A. Hodge, <u>The Day Changed and the Sabbath Preserved</u> (Philadelphia: Great Commissions Publication, n. d.), p. 5.

[6]Hodge, <u>Systematic Theology</u>, 3:340.

[7]Beckwith and Stott point out that there was a difference between the Jewish Hellenistic (Greek) concept of the Sabbath and the Palestinian concept. The Palestinian view saw the Sabbath for Israel only, but the Hellenistic view saw the Sabbath for all mankind. Thus the way Jesus spoke in Mark 2:27 is significant: the Sabbath is for all mankind, <u>Christian Sunday</u>, p. 147, footnote 10.

[8]Ibid., p. 11.

[9]Rayburn, "Should Christians Observe?", pp. 80-82.

[10]Reymond, "Lord's Day Observance", pp. 16-17.

[11]Vos, <u>Biblical Theology</u>, p. 158.

[12]Gaffin, "Sabbath Rest," p. 51, footnote 37.

[13]James O. Buswell, <u>A Systematic Theology of the Christian Religion</u>, 2 vols. (Grand Rapids: Zondervan Publishing House, 1962), 1:370.

Chapter 12

[1]Wilfred Stott, "A Note on the Word KYPIAKH," <u>New Testament Studies</u>, 12 (1965-1966):70-74.

[2]Reymond, "Lord's Day Observance," p. 9.

[3]Ibid., pp. 17-19.

[4]John H. Primus, "Calvin and the Puritan Sabbath," <u>Exploring the Heritage of John Calvin</u>, ed. by David E. Holwerda (Grand Rapids: Baker Book House, 1976), p. 48.

[5]Rayburn, "Should Christians Observe?", pp. 80-82.

[6]Reymond, "Lord's Day Observance," pp. 16-17.

[7]Rayburn, "Should Christians Observe?", pp. 79.
Chapter 13

[1]Schrotenboer, Acts of the RES, pp. 160-161.

[2]Gaffin, "Sabbath Rest," pp. 35-36.

[3]Ibid., p. 47.

[4]Ibid., pp. 36-38.

[5]Ibid., p. 43.

[6]Ibid., pp. 42 and 48.

[7]Ibid., p. 43.

[8]Ibid., pp. 38-39 and 44.

[9]Ibid., p. 45.

[10]Ibid., pp. 41 and 47.

[11]The other word for rest in Hebrews 3-4 is katapausis, the word quoted from Psalm 95. The word Jesus uses in Matthew 11:28 is anapausis.

[12]Ibid., p. 40.

[13]Ibid., p. 47.

[14]Ibid.

[15]Ibid.

[16]Ibid., p. 51, footnote 37.

Chapter 14

[1]Rayburn, "Should Christians Observe?", p. 83.

[2]Reymond, "Lord's Day Observance," p. 11.

[3]Hodge, Systematic Theology, 3:332.

[4]Buswell, Systematic Theology, 1:371.

Chapter 15

[1]Robertson, Christ of the Covenants, pp. 180 and 182 gives five different meanings of the word "law."

[2]Beckwith, Christian Sunday, pp. 26-28.

[3]Robertson, Christ of the Covenants, p. 183.

[4]Ibid., pp. 184-185.

Chapter 16

[1]A. A. Hodge, The Day Changed, p. 11.

[2]James P. Wesberry, ed., The Lord's Day (Nashville: Broadman Press, 1986), p. 106.

[3]Beckwith, Christian Sunday, pp. 30-31.

[4]Ibid., p. 34.

[5]Ibid., pp. 52 and 57.

[6]Quoted in Ibid., p. 57.

[7]Ibid., p. 59.

[8]Quoted in Ibid., p. 60.

[9]Ibid., p. 61.

[10]Quoted in Ibid., pp. 62-63.

[11]Ibid.

[12]Ibid., p. 65. Note also p. 155, footnote 8, for passages in the church fathers where laziness is spoken against.

[13]Ibid., p. 66. In commenting on some of the statements of Justin Martyr, Beckwith and Stott assert that there is nothing that suggests the gathering of the Christians on Sunday were hurried services before or after work. Rather, these gatherings were long and drawn out including social intercourse and meals (see p. 88). On the other hand, the Wesberry book accepts the view that from early on Sunday was not a day of rest but a regular work day so that the believers met together early or late for worship (see p. 105).

[14]Beckwith, Christian Sunday, pp. 67-73.

[15]Quoted in Ibid., p. 79.

[16]Ibid., pp. 79-81 where there is given numerous quotations from earlier church fathers to show that Eusebius is using earlier ideas and is not forging a new idea about the relationship between Sabbath and Sunday.

[17]Ibid., pp. 81-82.

Chapter 17

[1]Williamson, WCF for Study Classes, p. 173 makes the assertion that these activities should be prohibited on the Sabbath.

[2]Murray, "Moral Law," pp. 214-215.

[3]Ibid., pp. 214 and 227.

[4]Beckwith, Christian Sunday, p. 144.

[5]Rayburn, "Should Christians Observe?", pp. 85-86.

[6]Williamson, WCF for Study Classes, p. 173.

[7]Ibid. Also see Rayburn, "Should Christians Observe?", pp. 85-86.

[8]Williamson, WCF for Study Classes, p. 171.

[9]Rayburn, "Should Christians Observe?", pp. 82-83.

[10]Hodge, Systematic Theology, 3:342-343.

[11]Murray, "Moral Law," pp. 225-226.

[12]Wesberry, Lord's Day, pp. 199 and 46.

[13]Ibid., pp. 26-27.

[14]Ibid., pp. 135-136.

[15]Ibid., p. 259.

Chapter 18

[1]A. T. Lincoln, "From Sabbath to Lord's Day: A Biblical and Theological Perspective," From Sabbath to Lord's Day, ed. by D. A. Carson (Grand Rapids: Zondervan Publishing House, 1982), p. 402 notes the following differences with Rordorf: the Carson book gives an overall biblical and theological framework, gives a more positive assessment of the relationship between the Sabbath and the Lord's Day and gives a different view concerning Jesus' attitude to the Sabbath.

[2]Willy Rordorf, Sunday, trans. by A. A. Grahm (Philadelphia: Westminster Press, 1968), p. 301.

[3]D. A. Carson, "Introduction," and Richard Bauckham, "The Lord's Day," From Sabbath to Lord's Day, pp. 16 and 240.

[4]Harold Dressler, "The Sabbath in the Old Testament," From Sabbath to Lord's Day, pp. 27-28.

[5]Lincoln, "Biblical Perspective," p. 348.

[6]Ibid.

[7]Dressler, "Sabbath in the Old Testament," pp. 27-28. Lincoln writes, "Even if an appeal to the Sabbath as a creation ordinance . . . could be sustained, how much force would this have in the construction of a Sabbatarian argument? Does a mandate to Adam before the Fall necessarily mean that such a mandate is perpetually binding on all men and women?", "Biblical Perspective," p. 347.

[8]Ibid., pp. 29-30.

[9]Lincoln, "Biblical Perspective," p. 349.

Chapter 19

[1]Lincoln, "Sabbath Rest and Eschatology in the New Testament," From Sabbath to Lord's Day, pp. 198-199.

[2]Lincoln, "Biblical Perspective," p. 350.

[3]Dressler, "Sabbath in the Old Testament," p. 24.

[4]Ibid., p. 30.

[5]Ibid., pp. 24 and 37, footnote 31. See also Rordorf, Sunday, pp. 19-20.

[6]Dressler, "Sabbath in the Old Testament," p. 38, footnote 43.

[7]Ibid.

[8]Lincoln, "Biblical Perspective," p. 352 -353.

[9]Ibid., pp. 351-352 and 354.

[10]Ibid., pp. 358-359.

Chapter 20

[1]D. A. Carson, "Jesus and the Sabbath in the Four Gospels," From Sabbath to Lord's Day, p. 76.

[2]Max Turner, "The Sabbath, Sunday, and the Law in Luke/Acts," From Sabbath to Lord's Day, pp. 101-102. Rordorf agrees with this view, see Sunday, pp. 67-68.

[3]Carson, "Jesus and the Sabbath," p. 59.

[4]Ibid., p. 68.

[5]Turner, "Sabbath, Sunday, and Law in Luke/Acts," p. 104.

[6]Carson, "Jesus and the Sabbath," pp. 66-67. Carson points out that this does not mean that Jesus actually breaks the Sabbath but that he has the authority to do so.

[7]Ibid.

[8]Ibid., p. 89, footnote 57. Carson notes that the verb "was made" (ginomai) used in Mark 2:27 is used in John 1:3 in the sense of "create," but the two passages are different. In John 1:3 a preposition is followed by a genitive to show the agent of creation.

[9]Ibid., p. 65. Both Turner, "Sabbath, Sunday, and Law in Luke/Acts," p. 128 and Rordorf, Sunday, p. 51 understand that the Jewish people saw the Sabbath as God's special gift to Israel.

[10]Turner, "Sabbath, Sunday, and Law in Luke/Acts," pp. 103-104.

[11]Carson, "Jesus and the Sabbath," pp. 66.

[12]Ibid., p. 71.

[13]Rordorf, Sunday, p. 63.

[14]Ibid., pp. 65, 69-71 and 295. Rordorf also makes the statement that with Messianic authority Jesus broke the Sabbath, without however, formally making void the Sabbath commandment (p. 117).

[15]Carson, "Jesus and the Sabbath," p. 61.

[16]Turner, "Sabbath, Sunday, and Law in Luke/Acts," p. 105.

[17]Carson, "Jesus and the Sabbath," pp. 84-85.

[18]Ibid., p. 79.

[19]Ibid.

[20]Ibid., p. 91, footnote 74.

[21]Ibid., pp. 68-69.

[22]Rordorf, Sunday, p. 76.

[23]Carson, "Jesus and the Sabbath," p. 79.

[24]Turner, "Sabbath, Sunday, and Law in Luke/Acts," p. 108.

[25]Ibid., p. 111.

[26]Carson, "Jesus and the Sabbath," p. 95, footnote 136.

[27]Ibid., p. 80.

[28]Turner, "Sabbath, Sunday, and Law in Luke/Acts," p. 108.

[29]Carson, "Jesus and the Sabbath," p. 66.

[30]Rordorf, Sunday, pp. 296-298.

[31]Ibid., pp. 115-116.

[32]Lincoln, "Sabbath, Rest and Eschatology," pp. 204-205.

[33]Rordorf, Sunday, pp. 296-297.

Chapter 21

[1]Lincoln, "Sabbath, Rest and Eschatology," p. 205.

[2]Turner, "Sabbath, Sunday and Law in Luke/Acts," pp. 127-128.

[3]Rordorf comments, "Nowhere do we find any evidence which would unambiguously establish where, when and why the Christian observance of Sunday arose." Sunday, p. 177.

[4]Bauckham, "Lord's Day," pp. 233-235.

[5]Ibid., pp. 236-237. Rordorf states, "Is not their [Judaizers] silence the most eloquent proof that the observance of Sunday had already been recognized by the apostolic church and adopted by the Pauline churches?" Sunday, pp. 218-219.

[6]Lincoln, "Sabbath, Rest and Eschatology," pp. 200-201.

[7]Turner, "Sabbath, Sunday and Law in Luke/Acts," p. 133.

[8]Ibid., pp. 128-130 and Rordorf, Sunday, p. 202.

[9]Ibid., p. 132 and Ibid., p. 199.

[10]Bauckham, "Lord's Day," pp. 232-233.

[11]Ibid., p. 240. Although Rordorf at one point says that we do not know why the Christian observance of Sunday arose (Sunday, p. 177), at another point he comments that because of the Lord the earliest Christians were under an obligation to assemble on every Sunday for communal worship (Sunday, p. x).

Chapter 22

[1]Ibid., pp. 222-223.

[2]Ibid., p. 227 and Rordorf, Sunday, p. 208.

[3]Bauckham, "Lord's Day," p. 244 notes that there may be a deliberate contrast with a monthly day upon which the Emperor was worshipped as Lord.

[4]Ibid., pp. 244-245.

[5]Turner, "Sabbath, Sunday and Law in Luke/Acts," p. 132.

[6]Lincoln, "Biblical Perspective," p. 386.

[7]Rordorf tries to make the case for a direct connection between the Lord's Supper and the Lord's Day. The Greek word for Lord (kuriakos) occurs only in 1 Corinthians 11:20 (Lord's Supper) and Revelation 1:10 (Lord's Day). Since the phrase "Lord's Supper" was used earlier than "Lord's Day," Rordorf concludes that it is probable that the whole day upon which the Lord's Supper takes place received the title "Lord's Day" (pp. 220-221). He also concludes that the Lord's Supper belongs to a complete Sunday act of worship. He comments that if we do not celebrate the Lord's Supper on Sunday we have no right to call Sunday the Lord's Day (pp. 305-306). He believes that part of the problem is that people have understood the Lord's Day in the Old Testament sense of a day of rest sacred to the Lord (p. 274, footnote 1).

Chapter 23

[1]Douglas R. deLacey, "The Sabbath/Sunday Question and the Law in the Pauline Corpus," From Sabbath to Lord's Day, p. 161.

[2]Ibid., pp. 163-167.

[3]Ibid., p. 181.

[4]Ibid., p. 183.

[5]Ibid., pp. 179-180.

[6]Ibid., p. 177.

Chapter 24

[1]Lincoln, "Sabbath, Rest and Eschatology," pp. 208-209.

[2]Ibid.

[3]Ibid., pp. 210-212.

[4]Rordorf, Sunday, pp. 89-90.

[5]Lincoln, "Sabbath, Rest and Eschatology," pp. 213-214.

[6]Ibid., pp. 215-216.

[7]Ibid.

[8]Ibid.

[9]Lincoln, "Biblical Perspective," pp. 377-378.

Chapter 25

[1]Rordorf, Sunday, pp. 154-155.

[2]Ibid., p. 238.

[3]Ibid., p. 88. Statements made in the second century by Origen, Clement of Alexandria and Tertullian, which some have interpreted as supporting Sunday as a day of rest, are dealt with by both Bauckham, "Sabbath and Sunday in the Post-Apostolic Church," pp. 269-280 and Rordorf, Sunday, pp. 158-160. For example, Tertullian in De Oratione 23 makes the comment concerning Sunday: "deferring even our business affairs lest we give place to the devil." Both Bauckham (p. 285) and Rordorf (pp. 159-160) apply this statement as a need for

believers to assemble together for worship but not as a need to set aside the whole day for rest.

[4]Rordorf, Sunday, p. 83.

[5]Ibid., pp. 106-107.

[6]Bauckham, "Sabbath and Sunday in the Post-Apostolic Church," p. 264.

[7]Ibid., pp. 266-267.

[8]Rordorf, Sunday, pp. 162-163 and 166.

[9]Ibid., p. 167.

[10]Bauckham, "Sabbath and Sunday in the Post-Apostolic Church," p. 286.

[11]Bauckham, "Sabbath and Sunday in the Medieval Church in the West," From Sabbath to Lord's Day, pp. 305 and 307. He points out that although Augustine placed the Ten Commandments at the center of Christian moral theology, he spiritualized the meaning of the Sabbath commandment. He never treated Christian obedience to the Sabbath commandment as the observance of a day (pp. 300-301).

Chapter 26

[1]Carson, "Introduction," p. 16.

[2]Lincoln, "Biblical Perspective," p. 398.

[3]Ibid.

[4]Ibid., p. 400.

[5]Ibid., p. 404.

[6]Ibid. See also de Lacey, "Sabbath/Sunday Question and the Law," p. 186.

[7]Ibid. The authors of the Carson book say almost nothing about the present relevance of civil legislation (blue laws) concerning Sunday observance. Rordorf comments that provision should be made for unhindered access to church on Sunday for everyone who desires it (p. 304).

Conclusion

[1]As stated by Bacchiocchi in Divine Rest, p. 13.

[2]Primus, "Calvin and the Puritan Sabbath," The Heritage of John Calvin, p. 40.